On Africa's Lands:

The Forgotten Stories of Two Lincoln-Educated Missionaries in Liberia

Edited by

Cheryl Renée Gooch

The Lincoln University Press
Lincoln University, Pennsylvania

Proceeds from the sales of this book
will be paid to the
Students First scholarship campaign for
Lincoln University
students.

THE LINCOLN UNIVERSITY
1854

Published by

The Lincoln University Press
1570 Baltimore Pike
Lincoln University, Pennsylvania 19352-0999

Cover and book design by Marlene Lacy

Library of Catalog Control Number: 2014904438

ISBN 978-0-615-98090-4

Libations for
Phillis Wheatley and Anna Julia Cooper
who personified *publish or perish*

Contents

Illustrations

Foreword

The vitality of African American studies in recent decades has been remarkable. Scholars from many disciplines and perspectives have focused on understanding the character and distinctiveness of the black experience, and major biographies, reference works, edited collections of documents, cultural studies, and social and religious histories have appeared increasingly in published form, thus contributing to a kind of renaissance in the field. But *On Africa's Lands* is a reminder that there are still unexplored angles of African American studies which demand attention from both scholars and students. Compiled and edited by Dr. Cheryl Renee Gooch of Lincoln University, this book brings to life an important but largely unknown chapter in the black missionary movement in the late nineteenth century.

On Africa's Lands tells the story of James and his brother Thomas Henry Amos, who started out as free black farmers in rural Pennsylvania, and ended up as powerful symbols of African American involvement in Africa. The book highlights pivotal events in the lives of the Amos brothers, who were among the first graduates of Lincoln in the late 1850s, and who, under the auspices of the Presbyterian Church, nurtured and fulfilled dreams of missionary service in Liberia, the colony established by U. S. citizens in 1820 for ex-slaves and their free descendants. We are reminded, by the documents and Dr. Gooch's insightful commentary on the pages that follow, of the extent to which early black church and American religious history was inseparably bound to missionary outreach to parts of the motherland. Also, we are compelled to realize that the most important work on the mission field in Liberia was not limited to the pioneering activities of black Baptists like Lott Carey in the 1820s or white Methodists such as Melville B. Cox in the 1830s, as some of the scholarship suggests. Clearly, the contributions of the Amos brothers proved equally significant.

On Africa's Lands reclaims the lives and the sense of missionary urgency and compassion that inspired James and Thomas Amos, but there are other ways in which this book expands and enriches our knowledge of how events in black and American church history intersected with dimensions of African history and American history in general. First, we learn, based on James and Thomas's letters from Liberia between 1859 and 1869, more about the many seemingly insurmountable challenges faced by black missionaries, who usually subscribed to the white Western view that Africans had to be evangelized and Christianized in order to be fully redeemed and civilized. For the Amos brothers, those challenges came as they sought to successfully implement their mission duties with sporadic and insufficient support from the Presbyterian Church back home in America, and also as they struggled to reap a great harvest of souls in a Liberia in which there were three groups of people representing essentially different cultures and religious value systems; namely, indigenous tribal people or natives, black settlers or colonists who had been repatriated from the United States, and a mostly white company of missionaries. Unfavorable climate conditions, dietary choices and restrictions, threats to health, linguistic barriers, and conceptual conflicts also presented formidable challenges. The manner in which the Amoses met and dealt with such challenges is nothing short of amazing, especially when one considers the time frame in which they lived and functioned.

In an equally sensitive and sophisticated way, the story of the Amos brothers opens a new vista for readers to understand more fully the close and growing relationship between black Christian missionary zeal and the rise of black nationalist ideology and practice in the nineteenth century. Apparently, the Amoses understood the goal of African redemption in both religious and racial terms. In this context, mission work for them, as their own accounts imply, involved not only bringing the Christian faith to the land of their ancestors, but also a concern for the social, political, and economic uplift and empowerment of Liberians. The Amos brothers obviously felt a sense of bonds and obligations between themselves and the people of Liberia, and their activities must have grown, to some extent at least, out of a kind of nationalist consciousness, despite their acceptance of and reliance on resources from a predominantly white Presbyterian establishment. After all, this was a period during which black Americans typically felt a spiritual, emotional, and political attachment to Africa, and they realized that their own liberation and progress could not occur apart from the redemption and uplift of Africans. This outlook alone figured prominently in the Amoses decision to devote time, energy, and resources to missions in Liberia.

Dr. Gooch has performed a highly commendable service in compiling and editing this rich and informative volume, a work in which the voices of James and Thomas Amos echo plainly and eloquently in virtually every chapter. *On Africa's Lands* is a groundbreaking book, and not simply a luminous and exciting addition to the burgeoning field of African American studies. Dr. Gooch brings to its contents not only a thoughtful and informed perspective, but also a passion for detail and a recognition of its larger historical significance.

Lewis V. Baldwin
Professor Emeritus, Religious Studies
Vanderbilt University
Nashville, Tennessee

Chapter 1
The Institution Founded Upon Prayer

Prayer is a part of the physical foundation of The Lincoln University, formerly named Ashmun Institute. Buried beneath the grass behind Lincoln Hall, the oldest building on campus, there is a stone that served as the altar on which James Ralston Amos prayed the institution into existence. Ashmun Hall was the Institute's first building, both named to honor Reverend Jehudi Ashmun who helped to settle Liberia, the American sponsored colony to which James and his brother Thomas were sent to serve as missionaries during the height of the 19th century colonization movement. The American Colonization Society established Liberia in 1820. Its members supported sending free Blacks and emancipated slaves there rather than advocate for granting them full rights as American citizens. Presbyterian minister John Miller Dickey was one such man. He believed that an institution should be established to educate Black men to teach and Christianize native Africans. James Ralston Amos gave impetus to this global mission. Dickey's 1853 sermon, *Ethiopia Shall Soon Stretch Out Her Hands Unto God,* proclaimed that "the colored people of this country seem to have been sent here by Divine Providence that they might be Christianized and employed as laborers for the evangelization of Africa." [1]

Soon Ashmun Institute was chartered and began enrolling male students who would be educated to deliver the gospel to their commonly described "benighted brethren" in Liberia. James and his brother Thomas Henry Amos were among the first to graduate and emigrate to Liberia to serve as Presbyterian missionaries. Between 1859 and 1869 the Amoses wrote nearly 70 letters from the mission field capturing their voices which have been unheard, until now. Within these letters, James and Thomas describe their day-to-day experiences while revealing the challenges of working with native Liberians as well as the policies of United States based Presbyterian Board of Foreign Missions that both supported and hindered their mission work. In some ways the Amoses' letters were different from the often propagandized reports of the *African Repository and Colonial Journal*, a publication of the American Colonization Society that emphasized success and growth of the colony rather than hardships.

Before they became missionaries James and Thomas were farmers in Hinsonville, a community near Oxford, Pennsylvania, which free Blacks settled in the 1830s. Hosanna church was the community's spiritual center whose members worked with Quaker neighbors to help escaped slaves seeking freedom. Hosanna was a station of the Underground Railroad and the Amoses were active members of both. [2] It was within this stable community of farmers, laborers and abolitionists that Dickey chose to establish Ashmun Institute. Dickey enlisted the help of the Amoses, Hosanna members, and Hinsonville residents who provided money, labor and prayers to support the building of the Institute later renamed Lincoln University to honor Abraham Lincoln, the Emancipator President.

James was an itinerant Methodist minister when he sought the help of Dickey who then pastored the Presbyterian Church in Oxford to gain acceptance to a seminary where he could continue his formal education. He was also a praying man. Unable to secure acceptance for James to seminaries that denied him because of his race, Dickey began teaching James who walked four miles to and from Oxford at least three days a week. At the beginning of his walk James would stop in a grove to read the Bible and pray by a stone that served as his altar. Horace Mann Bond captured the nearly forgotten story of the unique place of Amos's prayer stone in Lincoln's history. He wrote:

> The very first legend of Lincoln University relates that Amos, then living with his widowed mother in a house close by the African Union Methodist Protestant Church house, walked each day the four miles to and from Oxford for an hour's instruction in the pastor's study. At the beginning of his walk he would stop in a grove, a hundred yards from his house, later the site of Ashmun Hall, to spend a period in his daily devotions of Bible reading and prayer. He knelt at a certain stone that provided a convenient altar. Four years later, when Ashmun Hall was being built on the same site, he noted that the stone of his prayers had been placed in the foundation of the edifice.[3] 3

Lincoln-Ashmun Hall. Lincoln Hall was built in front of and attached to Ashmun Hall until 1955 when Ashmun was demolished. Lincoln Hall, the institution's oldest building, still stands.

Hosanna AUMP Church, Lincoln University, PA.
(Photo Credit: Neal Hough)

The church Bond described is Hosanna that was built in 1843 by Hinsonville residents who owned some of the land the Lincoln campus now occupies. The heritage of Hosanna and Lincoln is intertwined. [4] Hosanna eventually became affiliated with the
4 African Union Methodist Protestant (AUMP) denomination, the oldest independent African American denomination in the United States. James and Thomas were Hosanna trustees and helped raise funds to establish Ashmun Institute. While James's prayer stone became a part of the foundation of Ashmun Hall, fellow Hosanna trustee Samuel Glasgow made and delivered the bricks for the building that stood behind Lincoln Hall until 1955. [5]

During the time that Dickey worked to secure the charter Ashmun, Hosanna provided a forum for discussions of issues of concern and interest to African Americans, including the abolition of slavery and emigration. Situated a few miles from the border of Maryland where slavery was legal, Hosanna's meetings often concealed fugitives. Hinsonville descendant Pauli Murray recalled this oral history. She said:

The meetings were held on Saturday evenings, and, ac-

> cording to some of the local residents, the church had been used as a transfer point for fugitives going west to Christiana in Lancaster County. Weekends provided the best opportunity for escape since slaves were off duty from Saturday noon until Monday morning. If they were successful in reaching Hosanna Meeting House while the meetings were in progress they mingled with the congregation and would drive away in a wagonload of free Negroes who hustled them to the next Underground station.[6]

The Pennsylvania Historical and Museum marker in front of Hosanna states that the church hosted abolitionist Frederick Douglass. The origin of the story of Douglass's visit may stem from his attendance of the 1844 meeting of the Clarkson Anti-Slavery Society in Oxford on Saturday, August 24, which he described in a letter to a fellow abolitionist. He wrote:

> This Society is very appropriately named; it is certainly one of the most venerable and impressive anti-slavery bodies with which it has been my fortune to meet. It enrolls amongst its members the very salt of anti-slavery wisdom, firmness, and perseverance in Chester county. The names of the Coates, Whitsons, Jacksons, Prestons, Hambletons, and others of the Society, seemed to be anti-slavery watchwords wherever I went in the county. The attendance at the meeting was very large; many had to stand outside, not being able to gain admission into the house. The Society got through their business at an early hour, to give place to addresses of Friend Remond and myself upon the general subject of slavery and anti-slavery. Our remarks were listened to, both within and without the house, with a deep stillness that indicated an absorbing interest in the subjects we were but feebly attempting to set forth. [7]

The names Douglass mentions, Coates, Whitson, Preston and Hambleton, are listed with the Amoses and Hosanna church members of the Glasgow and Walls families as Underground Railroad agents by the Chester County Historical Society; and the abolitionist Coates, Hambleton and Preston families had favorable relationships during that time with Hinsonville residents, Hosanna church and eventually, Lincoln University. [8]

Editions of the *National Anti-Slavery Standard*, the official weekly newspaper of the American Anti-Slavery Society, report frequent abolitionist activity in the southern Chester County where Hosanna is located and the Amos brothers lived. Months prior to Douglass's visit to Oxford, supporters were urged to use every available space to hold meetings:

> The design is not to travel over the old beaten track, but to hold conventions especially in those neighborhoods which have hitherto been entirely neglected. There are many places in this county, where the voice of anti-slavery has never been heard, strange as it may seem; where there are many who wish to hear, where the meeting-houses are bolted and barred, against the united voices of liberty and love. But there is "a house not made with hands," in which in every neighborhood we can hold free meetings in the free air with the trees of the forest waving their unchained limbs over our heads and the birds singing anti-slavery songs among the branches. Let no neighborhood, which contains a single individual willing to do anti-slavery work, be unrepresented. Let us put our own hands to the plough, and cultivate our own soil, with the determination to have it well done, if attention and industry will do it. [9]

Abolitionist and staunch emigration opponent Giles Badger Stebbins attended meetings at Hosanna where these timely discussions were held. He reported: "The Hosanna meetings were in a meeting house built by colored people, who formed a considerable part of the audience; we had a discussion of Colonization and other matters which awakened some interest." [10] On the eve of Dickey exhorting the divine plan to Christianize Africa, Stebbins's 1853 critique of the American colonization movement was deafening. The true objective, he asserted, was "expulsion of the Whole Free Colored population from the country; a scheme of wholesale expatriation unparalleled in its atrocity and wickedness" and "which, if carried out, would be highly detrimental to the best interest as well as the character and morals of the country" and "would be ruinous of Africa." [11]

Despite the often strong opposition to emigration, the Amos brothers and other African Americans consider it a desirable alternative to facing continuous discrimination and the threat of being kidnapped and sold into slavery. While Stebbins and abolitionists advocate for the immediate end of slavery and against Black emigration to Africa, James, at the behest of Dickey, canvasses communities within Pennsylvania and Maryland for support of the planned institution that will prepare him and other Black men to spread Christianity in Liberia. [12] The opportunity to acquire an advanced education and the appeal of helping to build an independent country governed by Black men inevitably convince James and Thomas of their missionary calling. On May 12, 1859, James, his wife Isabella and adopted son Ellwood Burton, and Thomas, his wife Susanna and their children, Emma, James and Georgianna, along with brick maker Samuel Glasgow, his wife Elizabeth and eight family members depart for Liberia. Fellow Ashmun graduate Armistead Miller [13] and his wife sail the same day.

Typically, emigrants received support for their voyages. The Pennsylvania Colonization Society paid $420 toward the passage costs per family for James, Thomas Armistead and Samuel and their spouses, children and relatives to sail to Liberia with the stipulation that the exact matching amount be obtained from the state treasury. The Presbyterian Board of Foreign Missions shared the passage costs for its missionaries by covering baggage and custom fees. The usual allowance of weight on steamers such as the *Mary Caroline Stevens* on which the Amos and Glasgow families sailed was 250 to 300 pounds per family. [14] Multiple forms of support were provided to free Blacks willing to leave their home country to populate the small corner of West Africa purchased for their relocation. The Philadelphia, Wilmington and Baltimore Rail Company, for example, provided in kind transportation for emigrants from Philadelphia to Baltimore who were destined for Liberia.

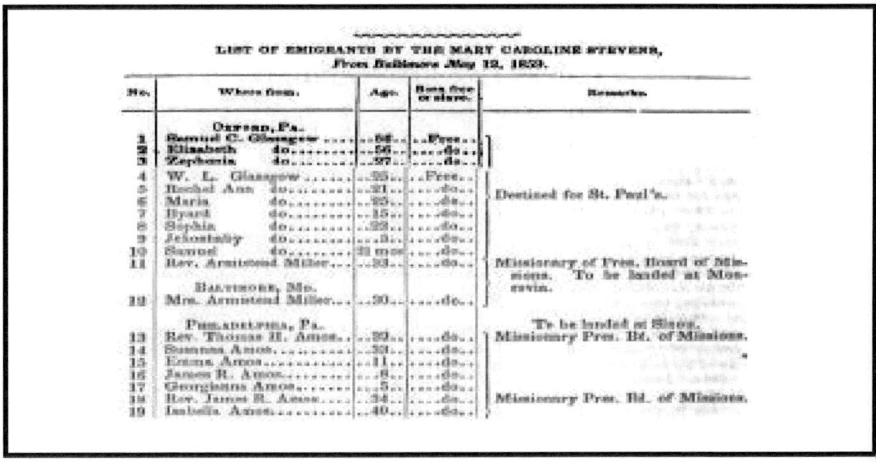

LIST OF EMIGRANTS BY THE MARY CAROLINE STEVENS,
From Baltimore May 12, 1859.

No.	Where from.	Age.	Born free or slave.	Remarks.
	Oxford, Pa.			
1	Samuel C. Glasgow	[illegible]	Free	
2	Elizabeth do	56	do	
3	Zephania do	27	do	
4	W. L. Glasgow	25	Free	Destined for St. Paul's.
5	Rachel Ann do	21	do	
6	Maria do	[illegible]	do	
7	Byard do	15	do	
8	Sophia do	[illegible]	do	
9	Jehoshaphat do	[illegible]	do	
10	Samuel do	[illegible] mos	do	
11	Rev. Armistead Miller	[illegible]	do	Missionary of Pres. Board of Missions. To be landed at Monrovia.
	Baltimore, Md.			
12	Mrs. Armistead Miller	30	do	
	Philadelphia, Pa.			To be landed at Sinou.
13	Rev. Thomas H. Amos	[illegible]	do	Missionary Pres. Bd. of Missions.
14	Susanna Amos	[illegible]	do	
15	Emma Amos	11	do	
16	James R. Amos	[illegible]	do	
17	Georgianna Amos	5	do	
18	Rev. James R. Amos	34	do	Missionary Pres. Bd. of Missions.
19	Isabella Amos	40	do	

Passenger List of Mary Caroline Stevens. *African Repository*, 1859, Volume 35, 171-172.

Thursday morning, May 12, 1859. Baltimore harbor. James, Thomas and Armistead stand among 150 emigrants gathered on deck of the *Mary Caroline Stevens*, a newly built brig soon to embark on her fourth voyage to Liberia. An impressive ship for which the American Colonization Society has spent nearly $50,000 to build and furnish, the *Stevens* includes two large iron tanks holding enough water necessary for the nearly month-long voyage to the West African colony.

Emigrants often celebrate their departures with sermons, prayers and songs like *From Greenland's Icy Mountains* that express Christians' interpretations of the biblical teaching to spread the gospel to "all nations" of the world. Originally published in 1825, this missionary song is popular during the height of the mid-19th century emigration movement. Sophia Glasgow, Samuel's daughter or niece, begins the song in which the Amoses and fellow emigrants join as they prepare to sail:

1 From Greenland's icy mountains,
From India's coral strand;
Where Afric's sunny fountains
Roll down their golden sand:
From many an ancient river,
From many a palmy plain,
They call us to deliver
Their land from error's chain.

2 What though the spicy breezes
Blow soft o'er Ceylon's isle;
Though every prospect pleases,
And only man is vile?
In vain with lavish kindness
The gifts of God are strown;
The heathen in his blindness
Bows down to wood and stone.

3 Shall we, whose souls are lighted
With wisdom from on high,
Shall we to men benighted
The lamp of life deny?
Salvation! O salvation!

The joyful sound proclaim,
Till earth's remotest nation
Has learned Messiah's name.

4 Waft, waft, ye winds, his story,
And you, ye waters, roll,
Till, like a sea of glory,
It spreads from pole to pole:
Till o'er our ransomed nature
The Lamb for sinners slain,
Redeemer, King, Creator,
In bliss returns to reign. [15]

Words and phrases like "benighted," "vile," "heathen in his blindness," and "error's chain," reveal the conflicting views missionaries often hold of the Africans for whom they profess a moral duty to uplift and serve. These words and phrases foreshadow the Amoses' attitudes toward native people they encounter and with whom they clash.

Facing fellow emigrants and well-wishers who have come to witness their notable embarking, the recently ordained Thomas seems reconciled to the contradictory mission conceived by his sponsor, the Pennsylvania Colonization Society. A free man of African descent who does not enjoy full rights as a citizen of the United States is being sent to Liberia to Christianize natives who are deemed to be in need of moral and cultural uplift. He says he is not from Africa, has not seen it, but is cheerfully going there to labor for God by spreading the gospel to people of his own race. James follows telling the assembly he is called to be a missionary to his people. [16] He and Thomas face a complex mission. Educated men, their prospects for meaningful life work in the United States are limited. Their country is heading toward a civil war over slavery, a human injustice which as abolitionists they have sought to undermine. For now they are called to a remote Liberian mission station where they will devote themselves to spiritually enlightening their African brethren while navigating mutually intolerant cultural differences. However they fare, whatever awaits them in the mission field, they are humanitarian pioneers. Their alma mater will loom prominently in the historical memory of Liberians and generations of African students who seek advanced education at the institution founded upon prayer.

Here are their stories.

Chapter 2
By Divine Providence: The Rhetoric and Realities of Missionary Work, 1859-1861

African-American photographer Augustus Washington envisages the freedom and self-determination possible in Liberia for men like the Amoses in his 1851 letter to the editors of the *New York Tribune.* He asserts that "if the colored people of this country ever find a home on earth for the development of their manhood and intellect, it will first be in Liberia or some other parts of Africa." [17] Within two years he emigrates to Liberia and produces distinctive daguerreotypes of the country's government and leading business leaders, some of whom with the Amoses conduct missionary-related business. These emigrants known as Americo-Liberians include former slaves and Blacks from the United States and the Caribbean.

James possesses similar self-determination mingled with divine calling to convert his yet to Christianized native Liberian brethren. Within a month of his arrival he writes his former teacher Dickey affirming his fervent desire to preach the gospel. The surviving version of his June 15, 1859 letter appears in Lincoln alumnus William Decker Johnson's early history of the institution. Within the letter James describes his and Thomas's initial work at Greenville, Sinou County, and the potential for mission sites. Convinced of their sacred mission, he says:

> We are happily situated in this place, and find it to be the greatest and most interesting field in Liberia. We are among the largest and most tyrannizing tribe on the coast; and they say that their tribe extends back to the volcanic mountains on the North and to the waters of the Niger River northeast. We have written the Board for advice in

> relation to exploring that part of the continent. Our school is full. We have twenty-four boarders and the Sabbath-school is very large. The people come to hear the word of God. Morning and evening prayers find many in attendance. We have access to many thousand heathens. You must know that even never tiring perseverance and undaunted courage without the special direction of the providence and grace of God could never have accomplished what we have been humble instruments in doing. [18]

Thomas's September and December letters provide details of their living conditions, encounters with other Presbyterian missionaries, dietary needs, and health challenges, namely the "Acclimating Fever," also called African Fever, a folk name for malaria. Poor health and scarcity of funds will be recurring problems for the Amoses.

Presbyterian Board missionaries were paid annual salaries that varied in different countries according to the cost of living and included an allowance for each child under 18 years old. James and Thomas likely earned between $400 and $500 annually. Their occasional preaching at churches serving emigrants yielded offerings that supplemented their income, although compensation for work outside the mission required Board approval. [19] Their wives were considered as associate missionaries and helped carry out the work that included converting people to the Christian faith.

The Board usually provided a house or paid house rent. Upon their arrival in Niffau, the Board paid rent for the Amoses until they were able to build their mission house. They received periodic allotments of food, clothing and household supplies and, as needed, tools and materials to carry out mission work.

They submitted annual estimates of expenses and food rations in advance to the Board. Allowances for medical expenses were made.

Most emigrants (clergy and secular) were given lots of land at little or no cost, minimal seed funds, and food rations upon their arrival in Liberia. They were expected to become self-sufficient within six months, a feat rarely accomplished. Often new emigrants were destitute, lacked sufficient clothing, and starved. The Amoses did not acquire their own land to farm as did some missionaries, a deliberate choice. As learned clergy they were most interested in educating natives and training them to farm, especially as an appropriate alternative to slave trading. The land they would secure for the Niffau mission belonged to the Board and was intended to support an agricultural training school.

As preaching teachers, James and Thomas will be strapped for money throughout their missionary tours and dependent on a Board thousands of miles away for basic necessities. Board shipments of food, clothing and supplies often were delayed and insufficient to support their survival. The Civil War crisis further constrained the Board's finances and ability to adequately support its Liberian missions. Unlike larger, better-funded Baptist, Methodist and Episcopal missions, the 19th century Presbyterian community of Liberia was relatively small, numbering less than 1,000 members. When the Board did not compensate them, which was often the case, Presbyterian pastors depended on donations from their small congregations for income. [20]

In September Thomas writes to John Leighton Wilson, the then corresponding secretary of the Presbyterian Board of Foreign Missions who along with a board of advisors headquartered in New York and Philadelphia directs and finances mission field work. Still exploring the country, Thomas describes his and his family's health and their efforts to learn the native Kru language. He says:

> I am happy to embrace this opportunity of writing you, as I thought it would be interesting to your Board to hear of our health. We have all had an attack of the fever but we are enjoying as good health now as we could expect. Our doctor has not given us permission yet to go as far as Niffau on account of the rain in this the wet season. Yet as you know, we hope however to go soon if our health gets no worse. We are making an effort to learn the Kru language. A native man is our assistant. We are thankful to your committee for their liberality and also to the treasurer of your Board for the favor we received from him through Mr. B.V. R James. We are not prepared to say much about this missionary field as yet for the want of time and experience. This you know but we can say this, that it is an inviting field and that there is much room for improvement in this place. I believe that the day is not far distant when God will pour out of his spirit abundantly upon the heathen of Africa. We are anxious to be settled in their midst where we shall be able to exert a greater influence among them. [21]

By December he and James are more familiar with the missions serving both emigrant and native settlements. They worry about covering their living expenses and request food, household supplies and tools. Thomas writes:

> We received your very kind letter sent by the *Ocean Eagle* also the provisions agreeing with the invoice contained in the same; for all of which we return our most hearty thanks. I wrote you by Capt. Alexander bound for New York early in the fall which letter I suppose you have received. I deferred writing you since until now for the reason that my

strength has been prostrate from repeated visits of the Acclimating Fever. I am now convalescent and think that in a short time I shall be able to engage with more vigor in that very important work for which we came. My wife is in very poor health. My children are recovering. Brother and his family are enjoying very good health, circumstances considered. As my brother in his letter to you has stated at length our views relative to the place where we hope to commence, the manner of proceeding, and our hope of success. I therefore will say nothing in this letter except that there appears to be an increasing desire among the native tribes, interior from Greenville, for us to commence our operations among them. Their visits to our house are daily and I find from repeated interviews with them that they have a strong desire to hear and read God's word. Whether their motives are speculative or sincere need not be a question with the missionary. Since we know that our success depends not upon, but upon God alone who we trust will direct us in all our efforts. I feel that the work to which we have been appointed, although a tedious and difficult one, is a most interesting and glorious one. I am persuaded that anyone here who enjoys the blessing of God's Holy Spirit must feel more or less the importance of this noble work disseminating Christian knowledge among the African Heathen.

We are at Monrovia to meet Presbytery and connect ourselves with the same. This meeting will take place in a few days. We visited Brother Erskine's Church at Clay Ashland last Sabbath. I preached and administered the Lord's Supper. We had a very encouraging meeting. Brother A. [Armistead] Miller preached and baptized 2 adults. Brother James Amos addressed the communicants. The congregation seemed to give that attention which the nature of the occasion required. I was in hopes that by this time I would have been able to have written something for the press but for want of strength I must defer on account of sickness and other providences beyond our control.

Our expenses have been great. House rent is $5 per month

> each. We have purchased a large canoe for the amount you appropriated for that purpose. We hope your board will be pleased to allow us to have the whole amount of this year's appropriation as soon as will be convenient for them as it will enable us to change our situation and our expenses will not be so great. We wish to avoid debt in every respect and we do not wish either to impose upon the funds of your kind board. I think that hereafter we will not have the necessity of making such requests.
>
> I have here given the list of provisions which we beg you will please forward to us as we cannot obtain those articles at the same rates here as they come to us from N.Y. We expect as soon as we return home again into the country and commence our work though we will not do anything pertinent until we hear from you. [22]

The brothers' attached list of requested provisions show their continuing preference for American foods and products including:

1 lb. flour, 2 lbs. pork, 1 lb. beef

10 lbs. tea green and black mixed. Best quality.

10 lbs. Adamantine candles

1 box chemical olive soap

2 lbs. water crackers

1 lb. indigo

2 lbs. black pepper. Not ground.

1 lb. olives

1 lb. Allspice

1 lb. ground ginger

1 bushel dried apples

2 bushels white beans

1 can butter

Crushed sugar

1 lb. fine salt

They also request household items and tools such as brooms, cloth, and dress patterns, spools of black thread, medicines, garden seeds and hoes. [23]

By December James is adamant about the direction their mission should take. A gifted communicator, James uses a well-honed sermonic tone to make a compelling case to Wilson for establishing an agricultural training school in which natives would learn literacy and farming skills while undergoing Christian conversion and socialization. Beginning what reads like an extended sermon, James asserts that a philosophical change in the approach to missionary work in Liberia is necessary to ensure long term success. He begins by asking "Why so many untaught heathen and so little influence going out from missionaries and Christian people among them?" and continues:

> I think the simple reason is that the proper mood of instruction has not been adopted. I have deferred writing you till now for the reason that I might give you a full statement of our views relative to our mission. I shall give an account not only of what I have learned from my own observation and experience for six months, but also the experience of men of long residence as they have related to me concerning the great work of evangelizing this heathen country.
>
> My connections before coming to this place concerning the enlightening or civilizing the African heathen were lst that the work must be commenced in the children and 2nd that the children must undergo a preparation to the reception of the gospel. Since my arrival here, every evidence

that I can gather both from observation and inquiry--substantiate the same.

I am aware however that it is generally considered that to preach the gospel to the heathen and to teach them to read and write is the entire work of the missionary. Anyone however who is acquainted with the present state of the African mission must admit that one of two things is true, that is, either the proper mood of evangelizing the African heathen has not been adopted; or that the missionary has been unfaithful in discharging his duty. I cannot admit the latter because in my view of human nature, missionaries who have happy homes and endearing associates would not leave them and come to this land that has proved so fatal to human life and fail to make every exertion to forward his work; and therefore I cannot think that the want of success in the great work should be attributed either to indolence or incapability on the part of them.

My first proposition is the work must be commenced in 19
the children if it is to become permanent work, and second, the children must be taught how to earn their living so that they will not be compelled to leave the school with the entire incompetency to resort to anything but the vague habits of the heathen. I have seen since my arrival on this coast more than one that could not speak the English language, read and write were taught in missionary school and have gone back into the habits of heathenism again. Not because it was preferable, but because they were not prepared to enter upon civilized life, and in my opinion never will be while the principles initially of the arts and sciences are excluded from them. Can such a state of things pass before our eyes unnoticed? Does it not startle us from our repose? Is this always to be the result of the lives and labors of the African missionary? Is the sandy beach of this dark continent to be forever whitened with their bleached bones without success? Are the benevolent Christian friends of other countries always to lavish their contributions upon these shores for naught and offer their prayers for the promotion of the work in vain? Is not the

African heathen a portion of that inheritance of which Christ by the will of the Father is as legal? And will not the word accomplish that whereunto it is sent? Yes. I believe that all this will be done. God will be glorified in Africa. But are not men the appointed instruments to do this work? God has not only set men over this work, but he has provided certain means for its accomplishment which means never have been properly put in operation among the heathen of Africa. And therefore I think that the work has been unsuccessful upon this simple failure alone.

I learn from reading one of the lectures delivered by the immortal Jehudi Ashmun in Monrovia at an annual meeting that such were his views concerning the great work; and such was his advice. Those who were present, as well as to those who should come after him. This question cannot be too deeply considered, whether civilization in some degree must not precede a thorough and permanent Christianity. It seems to me that it must in ordinary cases. The first lesson given to man in the days of primeval---was to dress the Garden of Eden and to keep it; and among the first lessons given him after the fall was to fill the Ground from whence he was taken till he return again. God promises a blessing in the 32:20 of Isaiah upon them that sow beside all waters that send forth hither the feet of ox and the ass. But alas!! The African heathen have not been taught this lesson. They know not how to acquire their living; only by following those rude habits which are as deleterious to the influence of the gospel as the darkness that blind their souls.

What must be done? How is this evil to be remedied? We must have a system of labor be taught in them. You are aware that it has been hitherto exceedingly difficult to obtain girls but God in his providence is removing this difficulty. One King or Head man of one of the Kru tribes has already promised to let us have six girls and seven boys as soon as our school is ready to remain with us till they become of age. And every few days we have different native visit with their children ready to enter them in school

> wherever and when it is erected. Again the work must be commenced in the children, both civil and religious. They must be instructed in the rudiments of agriculture especially, and it must be taught practically. Could we expect our children to come up after us and continue a state of civilized affairs if we should shut out from their knowledge the great principles of practical civilization? What would be the result if the American people were to exclude their children all knowledge of husbandry and housewifery and let them grow up entirely ignorant of these principles? What would be the state of society and religion in the next century you may imagine? Therefore shutting out these great principles will degenerate a highly civilized community in one century. Would not their introduction and perpetuation among a heathen people exhibit a remarkable enlightening tendency in the same time? Some however may doubt the susceptibility of the African heathen of the high attainments of civilization. But as you are acquainted with the African character, it would be unnecessary for my present purpose to argue that subject. [24]

James proposes to set up the school inland among tribes near the falls of the Sinou River most in need of basic academic and work skills. He confers with Liberian President Stephen Allen Benson whom he quotes as saying such a school "is the only hope of success." Impressed with the Amoses' innovative plan, Benson is willing to appropriate 300 acres for the school James says will provide education and work training to both natives and emigrants, many of whom lack skills.

> An agricultural school therefore will do more if properly conducted in advancing the work of civilizing the African heathen than any other kind of effort that can --put out foods. And not only so but it is the only thing that can be self-sustaining. And I guarantee that such enterprises in this coast would save the Board thousands of dollars and do much more in changing the habits and morals of the people both of the Americo Liberian and Native in seven

years than fifty years spent in the present system of missionary labor. Three hundred acres of the best quality of land can be obtained without any expense to the Board which will be sufficient to thoroughly best the utility of such an enterprise. And if successful will give one hundred students employment. And in a few years may so develop itself as to establish a permanent manual labor system in all the branches of mechanism. [25]

Liberia President Stephen Allen Benson (1856-1864) supported the plan for an agricultural training school that James and Thomas asked the Presbyterian Board of Foreign Missions to support.
(Library of Congress)

Concluding, he lists the tools needed to begin cultivating the land, and requests clothing for the 24 boys and girls expected to enroll. The school will involve a structured regimen including:

Rise--in the morning and prepare for worship at 6. Go to work on farm till 9:00. Breakfast. School open at 10. Continue till 2. Dinner at 3. Return to work on farm till 6. 8 o'clock evening worship Sabbath; one of us preach after meal--exercise--the other preach at one of the native town[s] and so alternately have preaching by one in the morning and the other afternoon. [26]

James says he and Thomas, who has cosigned the letter with " agree with the above statements," will wait for the Board's permission before starting the operation. [27]

By early 1860 they are still waiting for Board approval. Their jointly authored letter to Wilson in February reiterates their ambitious plan, this time with more details. The day before posting the letter, James and Thomas visit several native towns in the Sinou County area where they meet with five kings and amiably negotiate and sign an agreement to use land for living, farming and to operate their training school. These kings agree to enroll their children. The brothers urge the Board to support their petition on behalf of the Presbyterian mission to the Legislature of Liberia for the acquisition of 100 acres for the experiment. The modification from 300 to 100 acres may indicate their attempt to more cautiously approach the Board. Having farmed in Hinsonville, they believe the initiative also will diffuse the growing hostility between American settlers and natives. Undeterred by the Board's lack of response, they report:

> We have not only concluded I hope under divine direction to make our effort on the Sinou River just below the Falls a place accessible to five different native towns. We have also petitioned the Legislature of this Republic for one hundred acres of land with which to commence operation, the grant of which I send you a copy. A Resolution granting to the Presbyterian Missionary Society in the County of Sinou one hundred acres of land for missionary purposes.
>
> *Whereas James Ralston and Thomas Henry Amos have for and in behalf of the U.S. Presbyterian Mission in their charge in the county aforesaid petitioned the Legislature of Liberia to grant them one hundred acres of land for this purpose of establishing a manual labor school among the natives so as to evangelize and*

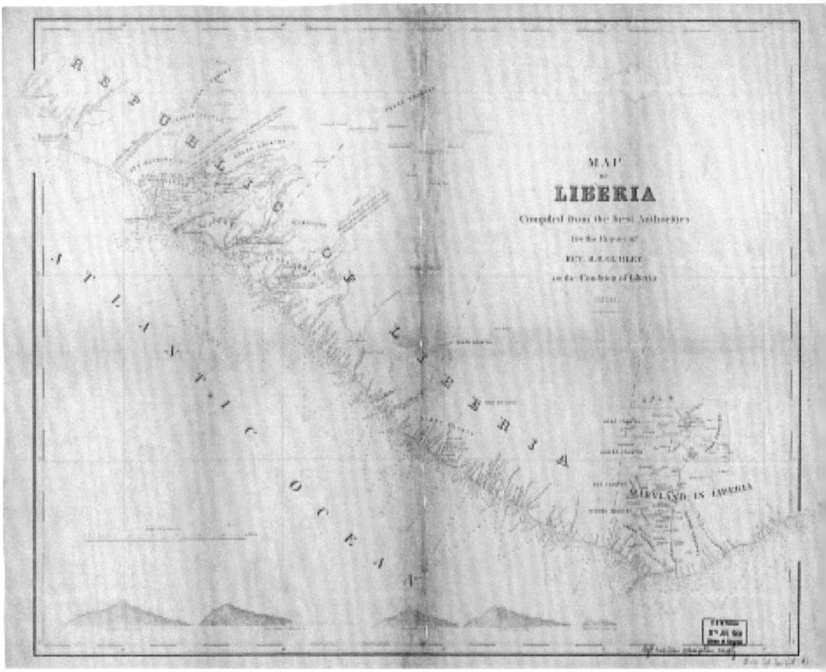

Map of Liberia, 1850. (Library of Congress)

instruct them in the arts of agriculture, to develop the resources of natives and to train them to the habits and usefulness of civilized life and the Christian religion.

And whereas we believe it to be one of the cherished objects of this government to patronize and encourage all benevolent enterprises that may wish to establish missions within its borders for the purposes above mentioned.

Therefore, This resolved by the Senate and House of representatives of the Republic of Liberia in Legislature assembled--That the superintendent of the County of Sinou be and he is hereby authorized under the direction of the President to have surveyed and laid out in the County of Sinou one hundred acres of land for the use of U.S. Presbyterian Mission Board. This said mission survey shall commence one and a half miles, or there abouts, below the falls or rapids of the Sinou River on the North Kessuen bank, and from a square block or track of one hundred acres.

This said Missionary Society paying all expenses of the survey.

Map of Liberia, political. (U.S. Department of State)

And when the said land shall have been properly surveyed and laid out and marked by the surveyor, he shall report the same to the superintendent who shall upon receiving the report, grant to the said James Ralston and Thomas Henry Amos a certificate for the said track of land. And upon the jurisdiction of the superintendent's certificate to the President of the Republic, he is hereby authorized and directed to grant a deed. Agreeable to the twelfth section of the fifth article of the constitution in his usual manner of granting deeds of land to benevolent societies and institutions in this Republic. Signed, approve[d] January 1860, A W. Gardener, Speaker of the House, D.B. Warner, President of Senate. The surveying of this land will cost thirty dollars.

This land is of the very best quality, the spot selected upon which to rest our buildings is on the most beautiful--in the whole country. The prominence is about 100 feet above the level of the river. On Tuesday the 8th --we went up the River and made the following treaty or agreement with the five kings or head men of five Niffau towns and after holding a council for half a day, which was exceedingly interesting indeed, they agreed to the following article.

Article of Agreement Between James Ralston and Thomas Henry Amos and the Native Africans: Sinou County, Liberia. Know all men by these present that Mingo Peter, Sharkeo, Soldier King, Manicus, Nynaker, do agree and hereby these present do bind themselves to let James Ralston and Thomas Henry Amos live with their families within one fourth of a mile from Swakia Town on the N.K [North Kessuen] and same side of the River. And that the said kings do binds themselves not to interrupt the said J.R and Thomas Henry Amos or suffer it to be done by any of their subjects And the said kings do further bind themselves to let the said James Ralston and Thomas Henry Amos establish a manual labor school for the instructions of their said head men's children or any other children that may be admitted to the school. The said head men do further bind themselves to let the said James Ralston and Thomas Henry Amos farm to a line that may be run by the surveyor of the county extending N.W. within one fourth of a mile of Swakia town and running N.E., E., and E. and S. as may be run by the surveyor.

And the said head men do further bind themselves not to so interfere with or disturb any of the lands occupied by the said J.R and Thomas Henry Amos or anything planted there on or suffer any of their subjects so to do. The said head men do further bind themselves to encourage the said manual labor school by sending their children and leaving them remain until they shall have acquired a knowledge of reading, writing and agriculture ---And further that the said head men will when occasion require assemble their people in the several different towns for preaching and other religious instruction.

And the said James Ralston and Thomas Henry Amos on their part do bind themselves by these present not to interfere or meddle with anything lawfully belonging to the said head men or suffer any one under their charge to do if in their power to prevent it. We want to bind them to duty by moral obligation instead of dashing them to hear the gospel and resume instruction. And the said James Ralston and Thomas Henry Amos do further bind themselves to instruct the children of these head men, and as many as they may be able if they will submit to the rules of the school) in literature, agriculture, morals and the Christian religion, and all board, lodge and clothe them.

To all of which we the said parties do agree and set our hands and seals this eight day of February in the year of our lord, one thousand eight hundred and sixty: Kings Peter (seal), Starke (Sharkeo), Soldier King, Manicus, Nynaker, J.R and Thomas Henry Amos. Witness, Ben Coffee.

This Ben Coffee is the head man of a large town on the beach. And he has taken the oath of allegiance to the Liberian government. The reason why we have taken this course is on the account of the hostility that exists between the Liberian government and the Americo Liberians and these Kings. And we think that this course will not only be advantageous to us but will be the means of making amity between all parties. Which we hold will be one of the principal stones in the building of civilization and Christianity
in this large part of the Republic of Liberia. Those men for certain reasons, all of which may not only be cherished by heathen, have lost confidence in even our missionaries. And therefore they were quite sanguine to know whether we intend to engage in either ---trade or the public affairs of the government.

It is important, dear sir, that this enterprise be established at the very earliest date. And although it will require more means for its establishment that ordinary mission stations, it is an experiment that cannot fail if properly conducted. Therefore I hope that it may have the prayers of God's people and the patronage of the benevolent. We are badly in want of a large river boat for the purpose of taking our things up the river which may be kept in continual use to advantage as there is none on the river. And we shall need some coarse bedding for the children. There are 35 or 40 boys according to our treaty with those kings that they give us if we may be able to support them. Much more I would like to write but the vessel is about to sail to Cape

Palmas. I must close. Please answer as soon as possible.[28]

Their next jointly written April letter requests money to pay rent for the house their families share in Greenville. Informing the Board of the debt incurred, they explain:

> We had to give our landlord a due bill for fifty dollars rent for house which we hoped to pay when our remittance came out. This due bill he sold to the bearer of this, Mr. Roy. He presented the same to me this 5th day of April for collection. I had not the money. He said he was going to Europe and thence to New York and that he would be in New York in August or September and that it would suit him. We did not wish to do business this way but at the same time we wanted to oblige him. If it is not amiss please pay Mr. Roy fifty dollars for us. And if you have sent money to pay our house rent we will refund the same.[29]

Nearly eight months after they propose the training school, the Board instructs James and Thomas to explore another place for a mission: Niffau, a remote, inland territory. Thomas, lead writer of the August 18 letter, provides a detailed account of their findings, including the social relationships between cultural groups, the size of the towns, the number of prospective students, and anticipated costs of operating the station. With the help of a native interpreter, Tom Nimily, Thomas meets with the local king who holds a palaver, a metonym both for a physical place for community discussions as well as a community discussion. For two days they discuss and agree on terms for operating the mission, including assurance that Americo-Liberian settlers will not encroach upon local lands.

Toward the end of his report, Thomas discloses that his 8-year-old son has died of stomach spasms caused by fever. Illness and insufficient funds are continuing challenges for the missionaries and their families.

According to the request of the executive committee of your board I made a visit to Niffau at the earliest period possible. I started on the 20th July but did not arrive at Niffau until the 13th August. This was a providence beyond my control. While thus detained, I visited the mission at Palmas and Cavalla which visit afforded me great pleasure. I assure you I viewed with deep interest their fields and manner of operating in the same. I have an account of all that I considered important to us.

I am highly pleased with the appearance of Niffau as a mission field and considered it a hopeful one. The town contains about 3000 inhabitants in my judgment without including the people at the plantation or the Batau people and New Wapee whose places are directly under the control of the Niffau people. And if these places are reached in safety by missionaries it must be by those that are connected with the Niffau mission, as they are quite jealous of their right to rule and their superiority over the above named people. For these and other reasons Niffau becomes the most extensive and interesting of any field in Liberia. From the appearances of the country for miles I judge it to be a healthy place. The land is moderately high, though not mountainous.

When I landed from the boat I was met by about 500 people who received me kindly and escorted me to the house of the king, who after making suitable preparation according to his judgment met me and treated me with all the kindness that I could expect from his royalty. I at once made known to him my business by bringing to his mind the circumstances of Tom Nimily's visit to the Cape ---on a missionary in 56 or 57. Nimily being present testified to the same and in evidence that he was the man brought from a testament and some papers that had been given him by Rev. D.A. Wilson in 56. A palaver was called by the king the same day and the following day. The decision was given to me which was that they were willing and anxious to have us come and build and labor among them and that they would send their children to school and come to church, and that they would give us protection against their people and assured me that we should be kindly treated if we would not bring other Americans there to sit down who would finally take the country from them, and that we should have land enough to supply us in vegetables.

We signed writings to the above mentioned conditions. We have decided to commence at Niffau our effort at once. The reason we make choice of this place rather than the falls of the Sinou River is we consider it the more hopeful field of the two.

Experience has taught us that we must be beyond the immediate influence of the settlers in Liberia if we would have a successful influence over the natives. And we found that if we went to the falls the settlers would surround us without any regard to our mission, or the bad effect they would produce against it. And as we were sent to labor among the natives and as it is our desire to labor among the heathen exclusively, for we think that Liberians have as many ministers as they need already it would be no special pleasure to us to labor among them.

The falls of the Sinou River is a beautiful field but only for the reasons assigned in a previous letter. We in view of all this have now made choice of Niffau. But it will be remembered that the expenses of opening a mission at Niffau will be far greater. Our school will be much larger than families. It will not do for us to turn off scholars in the first instance. Among 1000 or 1500 children in this town and this is a small estimate, 15 or 25 is a small--to be educated. This however we shall be better prepared to talk about in future. It is a custom to dash, as they call it, to make a present to them. Your committee has not advised us relative to this. The parents do not consider the food and clothing of their children. The dash money [is] necessary but only as a matter of course.

We have a doctor's bill of $50 to pay this fall for services rendered last spring to us and our families in the fever. I suppose you have received the order and letter of advice from Capt. Roye which we gave him reluctantly as it was out of our system of doing business. I visited Niffau alone as my brother and his wife were both in feeble health and still are so. The information you received relative to the death of my son was correct, though I thought my brother had informed you of it in his last letter. He died on the 15th of January from spasms in the stomach which was a consequence of the fever. He was ages 8 years and 9 days.

I and my brother if he is well enough will go to Niffau on the 23rd to commence our buildings. I and my family are in moderate health. We think that it would be well for your board to secure the land which the government gave for the purpose of a school as it may be needed in the future and as the only cost will be the survey and deed which will not exceed $50. We must employ an interpreter until we have acquired the language. You will please consider this and give advice accordingly. The landing at Niffau is very good though on the beach. Our building will be about 250 yards from the landing. From the river 27 miles. [30]

Thomas's October letter describes the time and expense of building their mission house. Yet to be converted natives are attending religious services and some parents allow their children to attend the school. There are more hints of impending trouble. Ship captains fearing robbery are reluctant to stop at the riverside area of Niffau, and the natives are not willing to accept "recaptives," Africans who are rescued from slavers and resettled in Liberia by the American Colonization Society. He tells Wilson:

Your kind favor enclosed with drafts and invoice of goods---I have not by me come duly to hand. We received our goods all in good order and were much pleased with your selection. We needed the tobacco very much as those people at Niffau seem to want it for--they do. I expect our dwelling house is very near complete. I have been from there a week for the purpose of moving our family today on the [names a boat, maybe *Seth Grassonor*] --in consequence of an unwillingness on the part of the capt. to stop long a naught at the point of land our goods. This of course is quite a disappointment to us as our goods are [st]ale or chiefly packed. We should have been much further ahead only for the wet weather. This however will soon pass off. We shall not allow any discouragement of this sort to hinder a faithful effort at Niffau upon our part as we are have been quite encouraged by the reigning earnestness upon the part of the children to learn and the parents to have them learn. We have been compelled to suspend our day school for several days to attend to our buildings and will resume it however as soon as I return. We will not board any until we move which we intend doing the first opportunity. We are afraid to risk our boat now as this is the tornado season. Otherwise we could move it all in it. We are not quite prepared to make our returns of the cost of our building and other current expenses. This we will do at the earliest moment possible. We hope your committee will not become impatient. I assure you it is not our intention to delay our reports not to misapply one cent which they have been kind enough to place at our disposal. Please accept our sincere thanks for the favor we last received.

You made mention in your last letter of the importance of the native language to us. This we feel and are determined to continue our effort for that acquisition. In our next letter which will be perhaps by the next mail we shall be able to say something of more interest. We have reason to believe that we have the Divine blessing upon us in our effort in this which we consider very important field. Religious service is well attended on the Sabbath day. Order is observed by all generally. We are all well.

P.S. My brother has not been from Niffau since he first landed there. We have not decided yet to take any of the recaptured Africans as we think it would not be agreeable to the Niffau people. [31]

By early December the Niffau station's house and school are completed, students have enrolled, and as many as 300 people attend religious services, although native superstitions persist. James orders a church bell and eating utensils, and requests medical books to assist him in providing care to the natives. The climate is comfortable; the landscape alluring. Writing over a period of several weeks, James's letter describes the progress of building their house and of native students' eagerness to "learn them sense."

> I have the privilege of writing you a few lines in reference to our mission. I am happy to say that through God's grace I have been enabled to build and complete the building of our house and other out buildings. We have not yet built the school house but we have a fine—piazza-- serves very well for the present. Building is very expensive in Niffau. The timber is often from fifteen to twenty miles that it is expensive to get it than bringing it from the States.
>
> Our house is 36 feet long and 24 feet wide with piazza all around it. Divided into eight comfortable rooms and large garret, a hall of five feet running through the center ventilating delightfully the whole house with the pleasant sea breeze. We are entirely free from miasma. The house is made principally of bamboo, except doors, windows. I did the carpenter work myself. And we have as beautiful as permanent a home of the kind as there is on the coast.
>
> We have been much disappointed in getting moved. The firm of Johnson, etc. have been promising and disappointing us for over two months, so much that we declined patronizing the said firm further. We lost at least fifty dollars last spring by the selling of our goods after they came on the coast. We shall expect therefore no more goods sent to us on the *Mirenda*. Our last came safe and fresh except the mackerel which are quite old and nasty.
>
> Our effort so far seems to indicate success. The Sabbath be-

fore I came home we had or near as I can count them about three hundred adults and children. Their very superstitions are in favor or lead them to favor our enterprise. The ambiguous prophesies of their oracles have been such as to lead them, further compel them to give us all the encouragement they can. For they say that "we are to make them rich" and "learn them sense." They have been laying their charms and gri-gris in order to make children whose parents are unfavorable run away from them to school and become American men.

I hope that God in his providence may so favor both you and us that we may be able to support a goodly number of these little creatures whose only hope is to be brought under Christian influence while young. As far as your eyes can carry, you can see the most fascinating prairies, hills and valleys. No swamp of any account or miasmatic lands. Our site is sufficiently elevated for pleasant and healthy sea breeze without so high as to produce chill.

Although the devil is an enemy to both God and man, yet is he often made an instrument for the glory of the one and the good of the other. My brother is going on with the school every day. The children seem very anxious to learn, from the feeling that more exist among them. Through the influence of Tom Nimily any number almost of children may be bound for five to seven years for the purpose of education. Nimily has given us two of his daughters and another has given one son and soon we shall have girls without bringing them. As soon as we can get a bell sufficiently large to be audible over that large town, there will go into execution a low-- probability any unnecessary work from being performed on the Sabbath under a fine of running to the authorities of the town. Two bells which will amount in balance--from ten to thirty six dollars. Please send one.

Our school house is completed. The children will be rushed in upon us and we shall have to take more than we have appropriated for, or turn some empty away who [which] will be regarded by the natives as a very bad precedent. Especially those who are willing to bind themselves for a term of years. I hope that God in his providence may so favor both you and us that we may be able to support a goodly number of these little creatures whose only hope is to be brought under Christian influence while young. "Oh that my head was--and my eyes a fountain of tears that I might weep over the slain of my people."

Our expenses have been very great. Traveling backward and forward and transporting goods and building materials and also keeping our sick families, especially our wives who are not yet acclimated in this dear place where you have to pay twice as much for everything as it is worth. If we had another large boat for sea we could save about $150 a year in transporting our goods which must be landed at Sinou. We hope that our great needs of one will excite your sympathies to furnish it for us. Please send as many common knives and forks, spoons, cups, plates as you wish us to take boarders. Some buckets, tubs and toweling will be needed. Please send me one of the best works of 'Malaria." I sold and gave away all my medical works when I commenced the study of theology. I find it highly important that I recall all my knowledge of medicine.

I regard Niffau as one of the most healthy places on the coast. Persons coming directly from the States there will likely have little or no acclimation process to go through. There is no miasma at all. The bush except just about the town has been all cleared away till they have entirely disappeared and the most beautiful grass has grown in their stead.

Here is the starting point for our mission. Tom Nimily says that they have seven interior towns stretching back to a volcanic mountain which has already buried one of their towns and from which also some of the head waters of the Niger flow-only one hundred miles from the coast. We are very anxious some time during the dry season to explore that doubtless very interesting region of the country. We will advise on the subject. As soon as we get moved we will send you the full account of our entire experience. So far as we have gone we have paid all our debts except a small bill we owe the doctor. Our buildings are paid for. God has blessed all that has come into our hand and all that has gone out. Rev. Edward Morris will be our agent to whose care our good letters, papers with all other remittances may be sent.

N.B. Since I closed this letter the vessel belonging to the firm Payne and Yates has just arrived here and will move us in a few days. [32]

Thomas's January letter describes attendance at the school and church services. He and James are having difficulties with some natives who challenge their authority, steal from them and try to intimidate them. The natives of the area are known for robbing ships, causing fewer supply ships to stop there. In spite of these difficulties, Thomas is mostly upbeat.

We are all safely landed at this place and are enjoying pretty good health. We opened our school for boarders the 20th December. 24 were entered upon the list; 14 for 7 years. Each 4 [for] 2 years each, the rest time indefinite. The age of scholars range [s] from 7 to 17 years. Their children are quite manageable so far and show signs of quick susceptibility. Before we thus opened our school ranged from 40 to 80. But when they found that we wanted them under our entire control, that is, the children, quite a different spirit was manifest toward us and our school. Though this I explained to them in the first place, but they did not think it would be carried out and their desire for pecuniary gain seemed to shade the work of a missionary--Our course of conduct among them has been plain pointed and resolute, and we trust pious. This now is pretty well understood by them. So they are more calm since they find they can neither rob us or frighten us away. We tell them we came here to learn them sense, as they call it and that if the Lord will, we intend to learn them something before we go away.

We preach every Sabbath. Our meetings are pretty well attended; say 200 to 300 in the afternoon. Indeed I would not say--if I were to tell you that we preach a short sermon every day. Prayers night and morning are pretty well attended by old as well as young. Good order observed generally by all present. We cannot tell what impression those religious exercises will make finally, but we hope, we pray, we look, for good and great results.

These people have robbed all the captains that have attempted to deal with them. This you may learn from anyone that had tried them. We wish to have little dealings with them, except to teach and preach among them. We have been compelled to send many in the bush for rice to supply our school and it will cost us more in the end than it would to buy it in New York. This may seem strange, but Niffau men are well prepared to teach this lesson. If they do any work they never know when they are paid. We, however, will not pay any more than we think the work is worth. This sometimes causes a great excitement among them. Their noise might be heard one mile. This we do not allow to move us from our course. God in his all wise providence has enabled us to obtain such an influence over them as that we can have order in and around our house. This they determined at first. That is after our families came here that we should not have. Having as we trust God on our side and some evidence of his blessing upon our labors, though faint, we feel encouraged to persevere.

You spoke of passing our account through the hands of B.V. R. James. This we do not wish if it can be avoided. It is as difficult for us to communicate with Mr. James as with you. We do not wish to multiply labor upon the hands of the officers of your board. We being at Niffau where our vessel will not stop, perhaps, more than once in three months we think it not advisable to have our business in the hands of any intermediate. If we were on the Sinou River or spending half our time in the court house and politics, that would do. [33]

The tone of James's February letter is more somber. Within less than two years of his arrival in the country whose beauty he euphorically extols, James wants to leave. His reasons: Isabella is critically ill and he is obligated to settle debts with creditors in the United States. He proposes to find work among "the colored in the United States," indication that he does not plan to continue missionary work. Perhaps his disillusionment is due to the Board's insufficient support for the proposed agricultural training school, or even the Niffau station. He alludes to the latter saying that Thomas, who is willing to continue the mission, will only be able to do so for five or six more months with such limited support. Also, the seemingly insurmountable challenges of working within the Liberian interior while straddling native resistance, and his own cultural biases and personal discomfort have influenced his decision. Living in a native house and exposed to the elements further weakens his health. He explains:

> I am under the necessity of writing you upon a different subject from what I have written you before. I ask permission to bring my wife to the States on the next arrival of the *M.C. Stevens* or any other vessel arriving about that time. It is not a mere fantasy in me to make this request. I am bound under both moral duty and obligation.
>
> 1st The moral duty is to save the life of, or to use all practical means, to save the life and preserve the health of my wife and myself. My wife is now passing through the critical stage and it seems that all medical aid will fail to restore her in this debilitating climate. I find my own health impaired very much from incessant labor, riding to and from Niffau several times in open boat; exposed [to] night air, sun and rain and sleeping in native house while building, much anxiety, etc. etc.
>
> 2nd Obligation: I am under obligation to come home to fulfill my promises made to certain creditors before leaving

> the States. In assisting to get the Ashmun Institute properly on foot, I contracted bills of considerable amount which were being paid as I could obtain the means up to the 7th of March 1859 when I repaired the books and found a balance due my creditors amounting to $1,000. I then gave my sellable articles of personal property which I had valued to a little over that amount. But--they failed minus $200 for the payment of which I begged my creditor leniency of two years labor in Africa as missionary and if they would keep their patience calmly, that I would, if God permit, come back and endeavor to make payment. I hope not to fail in my word, for it is my bond. If I cannot pay all this time, if only go and see them and show them a humble disposition to pay at the first possible ability, I will be well. The gospel will not be blamed. Moreover, I think that my labor for a season among the colored people of the United States, preaching to them and showing them their great responsibility. Other duty to engage in assisting the cause of missions in every practical way would abundantly pay my visit. Our operation here is more established and progressing with the encouragement of all who had any knowledge of the disposition of these people. In five or six months from now my brother can go with the mission with what help he can get without cost. Very well if God permit his Divine grace. [34]

The brothers' jointly written March letter to Wilson enumerates the difficulties of doing the work as instructed without adequate support. Their frustration grows when they observe the resources fellow missionary Bishop John Payne of the Episcopal Church of Liberia has at his disposal. They are enthusiastic about the school even though attendance has dwindled. Frequently, they refer to the natives in disparaging terms.

> It is with pleasure we write you, under such favorable circumstances as at present. Our school is in prosperous condition. The boys are becoming more affable. Several of them are spelling. Others know the alphabet parrot fash-

ion. The faculty of imitation is well developed in the native Africans. The number of scholars now in school 20. The prospect is that these will remain and that this number will be increased. Only one girl now in the school. The prospect for girls is slight. Meetings on the Sabbath are pretty well attended. The congregation are mostly young people. Tom Nimily is generally present and assists in preserving order. His brother, Jimbo by name, interprets for us. He understands the English language much better than Nimily. We have him employed at $6.00 per month. He manages our boat among our daily visits to the Niffau and Fish Town people who, if otherwise, would be very annoying. You may at once see his usefulness to the mission and we trust your committee will grant his support. You will remember that in my communication to you, I think of August 6, I requested your advice in relation to this matter. You made no mention of it in yours of October--in absence of which we thought best to proceed.

The town people have been engaged [cutting?] their farms since the first of January for which reason we cannot get our building finished. Except our dwelling house and yard and garden fences, which enclose about 7 acres of ground we hold school and meetings in our house and piazza. This we must do until these lazy natives get hungry again or else pay them much more than we would be justifiable in doing. We have to go some 6 miles for wood and we expect that in a few days we will have to go 4 miles for water. It is great trouble to get any now near our place. These disadvantages make our place more expensive. I make mention of them because they are contingencies that might not occur to your mind and which are hard for us to support out of our own means. I assure you we are trying to apply the means which your committee has so kindly appropriated to the very purpose for which they gave it and as economically as possible. Truly your advice to us is that we are to keep in the limits of $600. Now we can do this, but will this be to the interest, either of the Board or the mission. You are aware that schools on this coast are fluctuating among the heathen. This amount may not be enough to keep the mission in credit. I presume that we have the number now that you allow six hundred dollars to support. The question with us now, must we close the books or shall we receive 5 or 10 more and risk having to say that we are not able to support them the year out?

Bishop Payne tells me that he has 28 girls and 30 boys. He is but one and has all his diocese to oversee. We are two. Now, if he can take care of 58 I think we ought to take care of 30 if we can get them. If we cannot get them there is an excuse. But that we cannot take care of them or that we cannot instruct that number, I would not like to hear that. My brother wrote you in reference to this matter December 6, but as we have as yet no answer from you in regard to it, we thought perhaps you have not received his communication. We respect your experience as a missionary to this coast and hence do not wish to act arbitrarily in any respect as missionaries. We regard this as a very hopeful field. There is a large amount of material and an apparent desire for improvement upon the part of many. We try not to allow any opportunity for doing good pass by unimproved.

There is a great deal of sickness in this town. People die very fast. We are often called upon to prescribe for the sick and dying. I can assure you some horrible looking objects are presented to us for sympathy and assistance. Ah! To see a heathen die is not a pleasant sight. This is not the place for idleness. The sons of Niffau would beget the spirit of correctness--in the most--professor of the name of Jesus—My brother has the fever every other day. Mostly his wife is still in feeble health. You have no doubt received his letter asking for permission to come home. We are becoming very much in need of some of the articles named in our order sent last August. We are in hopes however that they are on the way to us. I am preparing a piece for the press which when finished I will send the first opportunity. My time for that business is quite limited as you must know. [35]

By April, Thomas is frustrated. The Board is slow in sending much needed supplies and money. The natives are uncooperative, demand money and continue to steal from them.

> We have nothing very important to relate this month concerning our progress in our mission since we last wrote you except that it is becoming more difficult to keep the boys in school then we had before and religious service is not so well attended. The town people are dissatisfied with our manner of dashing them as they call it-giving them presents-which only to do it when we cannot help it, and then only on a small scale; though certainly we have done it to the extent of our ability. They are not willing to come to church except they are rewarded with tobacco for their condescension to hear the word of God. Their inordinate desire for earthly gain will induce them to do anything that their unrighteous hearts can suggest. What they cannot get by cheating or stealing they attempt to rest by begging.

> We find upon trial that the head men are not willing to afford our property that protection which they obligated to do at the onset. Some of their people stole from us a fine goat and a number of owls for which we can get no redress. I do not know if this is a matter of course with the property of missionaries on this coast who are out of the settlements of the civilized or whether we alone are the unfortunate subjects of these grievances. Be it either way the wrong remains. But we may attribute it in part to this, using their own words; we have not dashed them properly. Now we cannot ask for, neither can we justify the act of giving what would satiate such avaricious gourmandizes as the Niffau head men.

> As my brother expects to come to the states in the fall I will need someone to teach the school. I fear that if all the labor devolves upon me I will not be able to do justice as I would wish. Please give me advice in regard to it as soon as convenient. We are becoming destitute for want of some of the things we ordered last August. Our health is middling. [36]

James's July letter describes the Niffau region's people, and their customs, attitudes and receptiveness to missionaries. He says the mission has the potential to reach, and, undoubtedly convert, one million people whom he describes as war-like, savage and in need of the Christian gospel. The tribes occupying the southeastern region in which he and Thomas are working largely belong to the Kru cultural group consisting of Kru (Klao), Bassa, De, Grebo, Krahn, Sapo and Niffu people. According to Teah Wulah's study of Liberia's indigenous tribes, the Kru were and are proud never to have been enslaved and wear marks of freedom on their foreheads. Like many tribes throughout Liberia, the people of Niffau resist the encroachment of the settlers, including some missionaries, and disruption of their way of life which profited from slave trading. [37] Following an inland tour apparently ordered by the Board, James reports:

> We have just returned from a tour among the interior natives, which indeed was very pleasant and interesting. There are some ten or twelve towns within four days walk from the beach. The bush people seem much more anxious to hear the gospel than these immediately at the sea. They are more ignorant and more simple in their manners. Many of them never saw the sea. They fear "if they come to the beach, that the sight of the waters of the ocean will kill them." Very few of them ever saw the face of a civilized person before, none having ever been there. Doubtless you are aware of the enlightenment that our appearance created among them. These people seem to be entirely ignorant of the existence of God. Their knowledge extends to that only which concerns their daily life. The following questions they were unable to answer. Who made the earth? The sun? The moon? The waters? Themselves? It appears that they have not read the first lessons taught by the "light of nature." Neither have they ever reasoned "a priori."

It is not with much reluctance that we admit that there are thousands, yea million[s] of our fellow men who have no knowledge of God, of themselves as sinners or of a Savior from sin? But how much more humiliating is it to admit that notwithstanding three hundred million enlightened Christians in the world and these people destitute of the gospel? Have they not precious souls? Would God not make the gospel effectual in their salvation, if it were preached to them? Is not the command "Go preach the gospel to every creature" an injunction upon all Christian people? Who is it then that cannot do more than they are doing to carry forward this glorious work.

Niffau is one of if not the greatest Mission field on the coast of Africa. I think it is no exaggeration to say that at least one million human beings are accessible to this mission. Although there are difficulties among them we have access to all their towns. Our ears are saturated almost daily with the sound of the war-horn and the furious yells of the naked savages. And our eyes behold the most revolting scenes of bloodshed and cruelty. Yet the God man so called The Missionary they look upon as being superior to them both in strength and knowledge. Consequently they will hear what he has to say.

It is evident that many of the advantages as well as the difficulties of this Mission were entirely hid from all mortal conception. Nothing was ever known of the interior of this place by civilized man. And every one having any knowledge of those on the beach looked upon them as being the most out-lawed wretches on the coast. Marine intercourse was almost abandoned. Whole cargoes of goods have been falsely retained and [ravished?] in this infamous place. They were distinguished everywhere for their fraudulence and prodigality. Their perfidious and avaricious hearts had driven all traders away from them. And notwithstanding this in time to prevent their entire nudity and destitution God sent them raiment as well as the gospel. Their darkest hours were soon succeeded by the glorious light of the son of righteousness. Though by them the light is not yet seen. May God of his infinite goodness open their eyes to see it.

More than probable, few or perhaps none of us who are now living will see the great and glorious effects of the work of the gospel among the African heathen complete, and the seed bearing fruit in this world. But in this we may boast, and who shall make our glorying void that we first raised the flag for King Jesus and proclaimed the glad tidings of a free and full salvation for the heathen, among these thousands of the benighted sons of Ham.

Oh! May not cold indifference cause any to think or say that the work is needless and had as well be abandoned? For if man withhold the gospel from the heathen, I have no doubt that God will, to our confusion, send holy angels from heaven to preach to them. His word has gone out and it shall not return void, but it shall accomplish the thing where "unto it is sent." Africa shall be redeemed to the everlasting glory of God. The seat that Satan has long and proudly occupied is beginning to be disturbed. He is enraged. Up! He stands furiously. Not that he is mortally wounded. But the nature of his pain gives fearful symptoms of fatal termination. Believe me. Yours in the hands of Christ.

N.B. My wife health is quite feeble. My brother family is middling. We have not received our orders yet which has operated very much against us in the progress of our work. If you will send us the--we will explore the heart of heathen central Africa. Tom Nimily is ready to lead us to the volcanic and the snowcapped mountains and many other places where he has already been. [38]

In October both James and Thomas request to return to the United States, urging the Board to suspend all efforts at the mission station for at least two years. The natives whom they say live in ignorance and savagery are hostile toward them. They are frequently ill and fear for the safety of their families. Wilson's improper management decisions, they insist, have exacerbated their difficulties: "Whereas if our affairs had been properly managed--these most disastrous results which are now so apparent might have been obviated to a considerable extent." [39]

Wilson undermined their efforts, the brothers say, by assigning them to the remote, dangerous Niffau area, and contend that he is biased against Black men. Upon the outbreak of the Civil War Wilson resigned his Board post to return to work within the southern Presbyterian conference. A former slave owner from South Carolina, Wilson once urged another slave owner to liberate her slaves and send them to Liberia. Noting his disapproval of immediate abolition of slavery, Wilson asserted:

> For I hold that every human being, who is capable of self-government and would be happier in a state of freedom, ought to be free. I am not, however, a friend of immediate and universal emancipation for the simple reason that all negroes are not ready for freedom, and would be worse off in that than in their present condition. [40]

Writing to the newly appointed Board corresponding secretary Walter Lowrie, the brothers delineate their concerns:

> We are sorry to have to inform you that a sad change has taken place in our mission, just such a change as might have been expected, pursuing the course that has been, in the management of the money of our mission. Just such a change as we informed Rev. JL Wilson would take place over one year ago if a certain course which we then hinted at was not pursued. And his superior knowledge concerning the management of a mission especially among those large tribes, and the peculiarity of their character which must be met by this missionary, and the one only course which the missionary is bound to follow and establish among such a large unrestrained and warlike tribe as the tribe of the Niffau. They have a thickly settled interior for

perhaps 100 miles to the avarice of those, together with theirs on the beach one are exposed, without even the means which we might and ought to have had out of the money which your committee liberally appropriated considering the money pressure. Mr. Wilson knowing as he did what was required in the successful management of our mission, and then pursuing the course which proved to quite averse to our success, gives room for use to entertain the strong presumption that it was intentional, that his assertion might be verified that colored men are not fit subjects to conduct the African Mission.

We cannot commit to paper at the present all that we have to say upon this subject but will only say that our prospects are all thwarted at the present and our mission very nearly broken up. Tomas [Tom] Nimily our greatest and indeed only patron has moved his family to the bush country and is there building a town some ten or twelve miles from the beach. All his children have left the school which consisted chiefly of his family. Our protection and safety in this place depended much upon his effort. Since his removal we have had a deal of trouble with those wild bush men. Mr. Wilson in his letter last but one promised Nimily a present. This he was anxiously looking for and this did not come. And more than this there was nothing said about it in Mr. Wilson's last. This we were obliged to remedy the best we could but certainly to our own loss.

We do not reflect upon any member of the Board except Rev Mr. JL Wilson. And we do feel that through his mismanagement whether intentional or not a great portion of the difficulties which we have encountered and are now contending against have--- Rev. Mr. Wilson knew as an experienced missionary on this coast, the result that would follow if we were compelled to draw our money from Mr. BVR James and buy our stores and merchandise from these heartless traders on this coast at an advance of two or three hundred percent. And then nothing suitable for persons in our health either to eat or--- At Niffau a vessel hardly ever stops that has provision for sale. We have been obliged, not only to pay three times the value of the articles but to beg the traders for articles of provision to keep from suffering. Whereas if our affairs had been properly managed in New York these most disastrous results which are now so apparent, might have been obviated to a considerable extent. But we are with deep sorrow are compelled to look upon the consequences being unable to remedy it.

Our health is so impaired through exposure, labor and anxiety to get and keep this mission on foot, that we do not think it would be prudent for us to make any further effort. We do not think however that our labor has been in vain. In the Lord, we believe that God will bless the seed that has been sown in this place by us. Yet we are of opinion that the best course to pursue will be to suspend all further effort at this place for at least one or two years. We are aware from the information we have received that you are pressed for funds. And we could not possibly remain here if our health would admit it without building a substantial house, to be exposed on the beach in a bamboo house where the salt winds blew as strongly as they do here and where the rains fall as incessantly as the[y] do, we are sure you will not insist upon.

All we ask is that you will send us five hundred dollars to come home with as early as you possibly can or make such arrangements for us as to enable us to come home in the early part of 62. This we hope you will not deny us. We wish to bring our wives and children as their health is very much impaired through exposure and an amount of care which necessarily devolved upon them. Truly our mission here has been a short one but we think not an unprofitable one. We knowing that our very best judgment has been exercised in all of our efforts in this place, and that our labors have been to the extent of our ability, we are satisfied that we will have the sympathy of your board in this last request. We remain your humble servants. We will draw on Mr. James no more than this year's money except further orders from you. [41]

Elder missionary B.V. R. James meets with the brothers who confide their discouragement. Writing to Lowrie in December, he says:

> So far as I can learn in the few hours I have been in this place from an interview with the Brothers from Niffau they seem quite discouraged in their work at that station. One of the Amoses expects to return to the U.S. soon and perhaps in Capt. A--from him you will learn all than is important of this field of their labors. At the request of the Amoses I will close up any account with the Niffau Mission for this year 1861. My settlement of the account with the missionaries will be forwarded by the next month's mail. [42]

B.V. R. James served as a supervisor and fiscal agent for the Board and had first arrived in Liberia as an English teacher supported by a New York women's charity society. Supportive of the Amoses, he suggests reassigning them. "If they are withdrawn from their field why not send one of them to Harrisburg. I only mention this by way of calling your attention to this matter," he says. "I have not mentioned the subject to them."[43]

Within less than three years of working in Liberia, Ashmun's first graduates are ready to abandon missionary work. James and Thomas embody contradictions of Black missionaries of that period: a belief of the supremacy of Euro-American Christian values and lifestyles. [44] They view native people of Niffau as ignorant, barbaric and morally bereft, and, at the same time, must continuously negotiate their complex missionary roles. They are educated, free Black Christian men working within a predominately white Presbyterian organization they believe undervalues their ability to conduct work within the African country led by Black men who declared upon independence in 1847 "the pleasing hope that we would be permitted to exercise and improve those faculties which impart to man his dignity."[45] Their acumen for discerning paternalistic assumptions about their abilities and, in particular, the New York and Philadelphia-based Board's limited understanding of on the ground circumstances in Liberia, is undeniable.

Prior to emigrating, even before enrolling at Ashmun, James and Thomas were leaders within a Black Methodist church which collaborated with progressive abolitionists to help freedom seekers. The Amoses socialized with churches within the African Methodist circuit which participated in services and activities such as the Big Quarterly festival. AUMP founder Peter Spencer established the annual gathering in 1812 to promote "inter-denominational and inter-religious unity and cooperation" among Black churches. [46] Drawing Christians from Delaware, Pennsylvania, Maryland and Virginia, Big Quarterly was a uniquely African-American celebration of religious expression in which both enslaved and free gathered for "song with praise, hallelulias and shoutings without constraint," worship styles that reflect African retentions. [47] The Amoses were familiar with, and likely participated in Big Quarterly worship services.

Equally certain, James and Thomas knew about Spencer's anti-emigration and self-determination ideals, given Hosanna's decades of association with African-American churches in Delaware and Pennsylvania where AUMP increasingly attracted churches to its connection. Spencer's commitment to social justice, education and spiritual uplift of African Americans resonated with the two brothers who were determined to be ministers of influence among their people. Convinced of the unique opportunity they believed Liberia offered them, the Amoses chose what Spencer adamantly opposed: emigration under the sponsorship of patrons unwilling to accord rights to free Blacks. In 1831, Spencer and his religious and social peers publicly denounced colonization as an "unchristian scheme" and the manipulation of the "Ethiopia shall stretch for her hand to God" scripture used to justify it, the same scripture Dickey used to establish Ashmun Institute. They challenged the pro-emigration sector to advocate for the extension of free Blacks' access to education and economic rights within the United Sates. They asserted:

> The present period is one of deep and increasing interest to the people of color, relieved from the miseries of Slavery, and its concomitant evils, with the vast and (to us) unexplored field of literature and science before us, surrounded by many friends whose sympathies and charities need not the Atlantic between us and them, before they can consent to assist in elevating our brethren to the standing of men. We therefore particularly invite their attention to the subject of Education and improvement… education is indispensable; our highest moral ambition at present, should be to acquire for our children a liberal education, give them mechanical trades, and thus fit and prepare them for useful and respectable citizens; and leave the evangelizing of Africa, and the establishing of a Republic at Liberia to those who conceive themselves able to demonstrate the practicability of its accomplishment by means of a people, numbers of whom are more ignorant than even the natives of that country themselves. [48]

Yet even the theology of the African characterized Peter Spencer churches reflected the complex identities the Amoses negotiated throughout their lives and particular circumstances as missionaries. The lyrics of a uniquely AUMP hymn reflect 19th century views of race and Africa held by many Blacks, enslaved or free, including Spencer. The authorship of this hymn is attributed to Spencer. It begins,

> On Afric's lands our fathers roam'd,
> A free but savage race;
> No word of light their minds inform'd,
> Of God's recovering grace,

It continues, eventually concluding with sentiments similarly expressed by emigrationists, namely that Christianity was a benefit of slavery.

> He led us o'er the Atlantic flood,
> That we might learn his ways.
> The children of that very race,
> Who gave our Father's pain,
> Are striving in the strength of grace
> To wipe away the stain.
> Who knows but yet in Afric's wild
> A Christian Black may sow,
> The word of God, pure, undefil'd,
> And a rich harvest grow. [49]

This hymn's theological assumptions, like Dickey's decree, and the eventual decline of the colonization movement, illustrate the limitations of proselytizing ideals steeped in conflicting identities and views of reality. The Amoses' conflicts with native people hamper their efforts in Liberia, as do Board of Foreign Missions practices, and the brothers' lingering concerns about the futility of their mission assignments.

Chapter 3
"One Double-Barrel Gun for Rev. Thos. H. Amos" 1862

Former Hinsonville brick maker Samuel Glasgow writes to his brother Jesse in 1862 describing his newfound liberty as a Black man in Liberia where he is spiritually free and unburdened by racism. The celebratory tone of Samuel's letter is typical of success stories the *African Repository* often publishes to encourage more Blacks to emigrate. Samuel tells Jesse who has chosen to remain in the United States:

> I oftentimes wish that you were here enjoying the same liberty and privileges that I enjoy. There are many privileges here for the colored people that they can never get in country. I wish that you and all of my relatives were participating in them. I am sorry to hear of the great calamity that is in the United States, at this time, on account of my own color; but, on the other hand, rejoice because you all have had the same opportunity that I had, as I now enjoy both spiritual and temporal blessings such as the colored people cannot in America. [50]

Samuel's liberating circumstances belie the hardships his friends Thomas and James are experiencing.

Thomas's house is damaged beyond repair due to recurring rain. Accelerating inter-tribal wars are weakening mission efforts. He and his family are poorly clothed and nearly starving. All of this foreshadows the inevitable: the mission will fail. Yet, while dutifully maintaining the station, Thomas continues to ask the Board for a furlough.

Thomas's fate pending, James is permitted to temporarily return to the U.S. so that he and his wife can recover their impaired health. Before departing, James observes somewhat improved circumstances at Niffau: the school's daily classes and church services have resumed. Having persuaded his brother to continue the mission for the time being, James departs for the U.S. During his health furlough he travels to Philadelphia, New York and Baltimore, and renews his commitment to continue serving as a missionary. He confers with the Board about plans to relocate the Presbyterian Church sponsored Alexander High School from Monrovia to Harrisburg, a large Americo-Liberian settlement, and soon is assigned to oversee the project. He continues to advocate a transfer for his brother to a different station. While purchasing building materials and stocking up on supplies for Thomas, he orders, among other things, *a double-barrel gun.*

***

 Writing to Lowrie in late February, Thomas pleads for relief of his destitution and permission to return to the United States.

> Doubtless you have received--this our letter dated I think Oct 23/61 in which we informed you of our desire to suspend our effort here for some time, reasons assigned therein. The rains have been very constant here for a month past and our house leaks very badly. I fear many of our things will be ruined. I have not got means in my possession to repair the house and if I had I conceive it to be a waste of money to build and repair bamboo houses in place as extravagant as Niffau.
>
> My health is something better than it was when I wrote you last. My wife is feeble. Today I have not one lb of flour in the house nor 10 lb[s] of meat. Sugar, coffee and tea are very nearly out and more than all this I do not know where to get supplied with these things as I have no boat and seldom any vessel stops here. And it is impossible for us to buy anything from the natives as we have no to-

bacco. I love the mission work among the heathen truly, but the burden that has rested upon me--The wonderful disadvantage under which I have been compelled to labor has made it quite necessary that I have the privilege granted me of a few months recreation. I am doing what I can among the natives, though it is not in my power to do much in consequence of continual excitement among them by reason of the war difficulties which exist between them and some of the Bush tribes north east and Batau in the south east of which I informed you in my last. This with other reasons assigned tend much to deter that effort which under other circumstances might be put forth with hope of success. If you have not received and written in regard to my last which was of the same tenor as this I hope you will answer this as soon as possible and determine as you think best. If you think I cannot come at once please send us something to eat, drink and wear. I make no special order just now as I do not know what course to pursue. I will try to do the best I can as God may give me ability. In him I trust. [51]

B.V. R. James weighs in on the state of the Niffau mission and the brothers' attempts to make it successful. He, too, fears that the mission may not be salvageable and urges the Board to reassign the Amoses whom he says "appear to be men of talent, piety & energy--and useful men."[52] Noting that James "has gone to Niffau for the purpose of trying to induce his bro. [brother] to continue at the station & make further [trial] of their labors at that place," B.V. R. James says, "Should Mr. Thomas Amos decide to remain at his station--I think I can send him a young man as an assistant that will assist him." [53]

Upon his brother's urging and prayerful reflection, and encouraged by of local residents' willingness to comply with his requests to modify their behavior, Thomas agrees to maintain the troubled station. His tone humbled, he says:

> Recognizing the wonderful overruling Providence of the ever blessed God bringing light out of darkness---I cheerfully submit myself to the blessed work to which I trust the Holy Ghost has called me disseminating the blessed word of truth--We have been much encouraged recently by the manifest willingness with which they have complied with the requests which I have made of them. That they should suspend their devil play on the Sabbath day--most annoying it being attended with unnatural yells that can be heard at a great distance, with a dissonance, differing but little from that made by so many bedlamites. And to add to this already strange confusion, the shooting of guns and flogging of women--generally crown their labors of the day. I make mention of this as it seemed to us that upon the Sabbath Day this unholy conduct was more usually aggravating.
>
> 56 To my request of their attention upon public worship, they have showed by their presence greater willingness to comply. And the children attend school more freely. I suppose that our former determination to suspend the mission has had its weight up their minds, as they regard it as a great shame to their country that the missionary should leave. The native Africans generally are quite jealous for what they regard as honor for their country. I requested them to roof the Mission House for their part that we might be encouraged to stay. This they agreed to do. We must not depend however very much upon what they say. Sometimes they comply, often they fail to comply. They say I must not leave them. Of course I held them in suspense until I received your last. This time they sent several persons to beg me. Since I have informed them of our intention they are quite satisfied, and perhaps they will conduct themselves better toward us for the time. --our earnest prayer is that God through our instrumentality by the efficient agency, his Holy Spirit will wake some of them in his good time from their Death sleep in sin and degradation. [54]

His enthusiasm seemingly renewed, Thomas requests a boat, dictionary and medicines. He advises the Board:

> Should you conclude to put up a permanent building at this place, you had better not put it off, as it will require considerable time to do it. I would recommend that you send the buildings out already fitted as you can have the work done much cheaper there than you can get it done here. A good boat I must have. I cannot get along very well without one. I want with it a good sail--a light chain and anchor. The chain would be not less than 10 fathom---as dependable to this mission for the safety, comfort--I believe all your letters have been received though it is quite difficult for us to answer letters from this place. It has cost $4.00 to mail one letter---I send my order with this which I hope you will forward to me at the earliest convenience. I wish my brother to buy some items which I did not put on the order which he will leave at your office to send with the rest. You will please send our medicines which he will name---The book you sent some months since we have placed in the mission library as you gave us permission to do. We thank you very much for them. I would like very much to have a dictionary. [55]

Awaiting his ship, literal and proverbial, James has a lot on his mind. The failed Niffau mission still looming, he ponders another way to fulfill his missionary calling. For now, that other way appears to be finding a new site for the Alexander High School and supervising its construction. He raised funds to establish Ashmun Institute where he superintended its first classroom building; he could oversee the school's construction and perhaps direct the school. Still, he wonders about Isabella's health, his adopted son Ellwood's wellbeing and his own in this Black governed county to which he has emigrated in search of a life unburdened by discrimination. Having convinced Thomas to maintain the troubled Niffau station for the time being, he needs to secure another assignment while assuring the Board that he and Thomas intend to fulfill their commitments. He tells Lowrie:

> My silence has been in consequence of being in wait for several months for an opportunity get to New York during which time I have been very busily engaged in the Harrisburg mission. And in consideration of the great success which has attended my business here, I seem to feel that God has overruled--my long detention to the good of this much crippled mission.
>
> On the reception of your last which related to the continuance or dissolution of the Niffau Mission, I after having made it a subject of deep consideration and prayer thought best to return and consult my Brother if it were possible to continue it which I did and found him perfectly willing to remain and anxious for the Mission to be continued. The School is going on daily and preaching and sabbath school regular. I preached several times during my stay. While we have no very distinct marks of the outpouring of God's special grace among the heathen, yet we have great reason to hope that there is much interest cherished by them, which doubtless will lead very soon to visible evidence of the work of God's Holy Spirit began in some of them. At my return from Niffau to Monrovia two days ago I met with Captain--just out from New York. I immediately arranged passage with him, but have to remain this month before he is ready to leave the coast. This is my first opportunity since I got permission to leave work here and return to New York except by way of England which way I should gladly have gone but for the great expense. Lord willing I shall be in New York in July. Further particulars I will relate when I come to you. [56]

The 1862 *Annual Report of the Board of Foreign Missions of the Presbyterian Church* provides additional details about James's trip to the United States for health leave, and his decision to withdraw from the Niffau mission and then assume work on the temporarily suspended Alexander High School. According to the report:

It was therefore decided not to resume the school till a suitable building could be erected on the St. Paul's river at the head of the tide water, twenty miles from Monrovia. Circumstances were favourable commencing the building at once. The health of Rev. James R. Amos and that of his wife had suffered so severely at Niffau that he was obliged to return to the United States. While waiting for a ship at Monrovia he thoroughly examined the localities at the head of the tide water on the St. Paul's. His report in favour of this position for the High School agreed with the opinions heretofore expressed by the Rev. D.A. Wilson, and Rev. Edwin T. Williams, while in the service of the Board. The voyage to the United States had restored the health of Mr. Amos, and he was anxious to return to any station in Africa where he could be useful. He is a practical carpenter, and has had experience in various other kinds of work. After full and repeated interviews with him, it was deemed important to place under his direction the building for the High School. He returned to Liberia in November, furnished with supplies that will go far to meet the entire expense of a brick building. He will employ his Sabbaths in preaching at different settlements within reach of the station. [57]

The *Annual Report* and James's April letter expose the differences between the Board and James about work for which he is best suited, and his growing unease about the nature of those assignments. The *Annual Report* describes James as "anxious to return to any station in Africa where he could be useful," and as "a practical carpenter" who is experienced "in various other kinds of work." [58] However, the man whose intelligence and eloquence so impressed Dickey to attempt enrolling him in several institutions, including Princeton Theological Seminary, James's talents surpass simple carpentry.

James possessed some formal education when he met Dickey in 1852 and stated his desire to attend a seminary. He and his brother likely attended Blair Hall, a school operated by the Faggs Manor Presbyterian Church, a few miles from Hinsonville. Reverend Alfred Hamilton, then pastor of Faggs Manor, opened and directed the academy for males from 1849 until 1855. He and Dickey, both Presbyterians in the Oxford area, were colleagues. Dickey delivered the prayer of dedication for the new Faggs Manor church building in December of 1846. Hamilton probably introduced James to Dickey. [59] Convinced of his ability, Dickey sends him to interview with Charles Hodge of the Princeton Seminary, a former teacher who declines to admit James because he has no formal educational credentials. "It strikes me that he falls under the provision for "extraordinary cases," Hodge tells Dickey. "I think it would be a waste of time to let him study Latin & Greek." [60] Hodge suggests a basic education and then a program of study in theology which Dickey arranges, first enrolling James in a Presbyterian academy where he works as a custodian while surreptitiously continuing his studies. After white students complain of his presence, he is withdrawn; an injustice that prods Dickey to forge ahead with establishing an institute where "extraordinary" men like James can pursue a theological education unhindered. Meanwhile, Dickey arranges for James to study at the Presbyterian Institute in Philadelphia, the school conducted by Reverend Lyman Coleman, an esteemed Presbyterian professor and scholar. James enrolls there during the 1853-1854 and 1854-1855 terms. [61]

During his three years at Ashmun, James satisfies the requirements of the rigorous curriculum that includes spelling, reading, penmanship, geography, general history, English grammar, composition, elocution, and mathematics, the Hebrew, Greek and Latin languages, church history and theology. [62]

While mastering these subjects, including Greek and Latin which Hodge predicted "a waste of time," James serves for two years as pastor of the First African Presbyterian in Reading, PA, under the auspices of the Pennsylvania Presbyterian Presbytery which through Ashmun provided seminary students to serve area Black churches. During these years of theological study and training, he continues as a member of Hosanna and working with an experienced, well-informed Quaker-led abolitionist network to aid freedom seekers. James Ralston Amos is a man far more complex than the "practical carpenter" the *Annual Report* describes.

***

Residing temporarily in Philadelphia, James visits Ashmun Institute and his former Hinsonville neighborhood, connecting with classmates and friends. He corresponds often with the Board about the construction project that he hopes to direct, and suggests that Thomas be reassigned to Careysburg, a large Americo-Liberian settlement near Monrovia. Given the frequency of his and Thomas' requests for reassignment, the brothers evidently discussed this strategy before James left Liberia. They looked out for one another. In early September James writes:

> I am just returned from a visit to Oxford and the Ashmun Institute. Had the pleasure of seeing many of my friends, most of whom I found well. I should have gone on to New York but thinking that I might save something by writing instead of going. I will await your answer. I hope that the members of the board who were at the native places have returned with renewed health. I hope also that the committee will favor my proposition in reference to my mission on the St. Paul's River. If any further information is required by the committee on the budget I will be happy to give all that I can. I am positive that a moral enterprise may be established there and also that no place claims our

> sympathies more. God has abundantly blessed my labor there already. And I hope that I will not be prevented from going back. I hope that there will be no possible hesitation on the part of the committee of establishing the Alexander High School and the whole entire enterprise at that place St. Paul's River head of navigation.
>
> Please inform me what will be done for Niffau. I think it better for my brother not to come to the United States at this present time. If his family's health will admit, why not send him to Careysburg. There is a most fertile field and one that is suffering for want of an intelligent and energetic missionary. I am decided by information--concentrating our missions for the present to Montserrado County until we get a better state of things existing in our mission--Please inform me if any vessel will leave New York this month for Liberia as I wish to write the first possible opportunity. I wish to return in the *M.C. Stevens* first of November [when] she leaves Baltimore. [63]

Once the Board decides to relocate the school to Harrisburg and appoints James to supervise the construction, he develops architectural drawings and heads to New York. Buoyed by these favorable developments, he says:

> Yours of the 9th is at hand. I am much pleased with the report of your committee. I think that they have wisely decided in regard to--Niffau and Harrisburg. I am at last highly gratified that I have the honor of continued favor of the committee. I beg you--that I may continue to--calling of God in Christ--I will--of a draft of the mission house and at the building---But I think it desirable--to build both as there is good brick clay on the ground. Therefore I will bring a diagram of both kinds of building. I expect to be at New York by Saturday the 20th of September providence providing. [64]
>
> Meanwhile, Thomas tries to maintain the mission in spite

of exhaustion, mounting bills, and spoiled food shipped by the Board. He attends to sick natives and requests more medicines. His anxiety is apparent throughout his monthly work report:

> Dear sir yours of April and May came duly to hand with goods agreeable to invoice part of which are now at our station Niffau. The balance, I am now at this place with a hired boat to take to our place. I have not yet repaired the house, but I think that I have goods enough now on hand to do it. I have given to Capt. G. W. Hall of the Brig--an order for Mr. B.V.R James to amount $113.00.
>
> I have bought other goods for the purpose of repairs as the above amount was not sufficient for these. However, I have paid I think to the amount of about forty of forty-five dollars. I have not at the present the bills before me. I will also give an order on Mr. James for boat-hire for the transporting of goods. The contingent expenses I will expect the board to pay. I do not know at present what they will be. But I assure you I will present no unnecessary bills. Perhaps the amount in all will not exceed what you have expressed a willingness to pay.
>
> I will not send an order with this for next year as I do not know what arrangement you will make with my brother James. If you send out a house soon you will send provisions as I will have to board the workmen. If you do not receive an order from me in time you will please send us such articles of provisions as you think are needed most. If my brother is coming back to Niffau I leave the selection of the order to him. We want a stove suitable for baking and the like, not a regular cooking stove, shovel and tongs.
>
> Our health is middling at present though we are not well. I expect to get a teacher soon agreeable to a letter from Mr. James. The labor is too great for me alone though I have kept up the school and preached regularly every Sabbath. The school varies from ten to fifteen. We have two boarders. We would not dismiss them as we think we may succeed in giving them an English education. I hope you will

> appropriate for their board.
>
> Their attendance upon divine worship is not very encouraging though there are always some present. I preach to many in the town who never come to the house. I am sorry you did not send me some medicines. I have so much doctoring to do among the natives that I am merely out of them. The people around us at present are quiet in comparison of what they were sometime back.
>
> We just received the provisions which were ordered from Monrovia at the same time the order was sent to New York last week, and they were all spoiled. We suffered much for them, but through the mercy of God we did not perish. I will write you more fully when I return home and my press of anxieties a little subsides. I am now much concerned about getting home and getting our place built in order. [65]

64 By late October James is busily purchasing materials and supplies and preparing to return to Liberia. Writing from Baltimore, he delineates some of the expenses:

> I received yours of the 30th today. Your change of the model of the building no doubt will make it more convenient. I will make the very best effort possible to put up such a building at the least expense, but taking into account the extreme prices of merchandise I shall fall very short. Tobacco is almost double the price that we calculated, and yet must have it for it is the main article for building trade and we can realize on it about 75 or 100 percent. I must have one small hoe head of tobacco which will cost at the lowest market price 22 cts. 1000 pounds at--$240. You gave me an order for 14--in tobacco which is less [than] $100. I shall be under the necessity of asking your Committee for one hundred dollars more. For it will be judicious to take that much tobacco out. Such a house can only be built for that amount of money by taking the advantage of getting high price for the merchandise. And the prices make it necessary for you to send me an order for one hundred

> dollars more. [66]

Responding to his brother's request for food and supplies, he explains:

> I received a letter from Brother Thomas on the 24th. He writes me that he has not made out any order for the beginning of the coming year and he wishes me to make one for him. I therefore will order him the following goods which you may either send out in the *Stevens* or when you send out the next remittance. [67]

> These goods include barrels of flour, mess pork, dry herrings, 100 lbs of ham, sauerkraut, one can of butter, tobacco, various fabrics, combs, mitts, a cotton umbrella, one dozen padlocks, one dozen knives and forks, one box of cigars, one business suit and "one double-barrel gun for Rev. Thos. H. Amos." [68] He concludes saying that this "order sent to Monrovia for him will save him from laying out his supplies till spring," and that "*The Stevens* will not sail till the 12th of November." [69]

James's November letters before departing for Liberia further delineate the expenses for the construction project and supplies for himself and Thomas, apparently in response to Board scrutiny.

> I have just finished bringing up mine and my brother's goods. I think that I have been very successful taking the oppressing times into consideration. I have all that I need for the present, for carrying out your requested, the Alexander High School. I had two hundred dollars of my own money which I gladly put to the six hundred dollars which you allowed me. And had I not had that amount I should have fallen short on account of the exceeding high prices of things. My brother's goods and effects amounted to one hundred and eight dollars. Before I leave I will send you the exact accounts of the goods and effects which I have bought. I have not gone over what you allowed. I

> write more hastily so that if you have my future request you will have time to write. One vessel will sail on Saturday morning. [70]

His continuing concern for Thomas's safety is evident in the letter's closing: "My brother is yet at Niffau awaiting your advice which I suppose you have sent him." [71] Their supply orders reveal as much about their tenuous circumstances as their families' dietary preferences that include meat, fish, ham, flour, butter, lard, crackers and bubble gum. [72]

James returns to Monrovia in late December, a trip that took 34 days. He is anxious to begin work on the Alexander High School building. Fellow emigrant and now successful businessman Samuel Glasgow is contracted to provide the bricks. Thomas's long awaited reassignment has been approved. The brothers' circumstances appear to be improving.

> Through the mercy and divine providence I am once more in the land of my mission work. We arrived yesterday 2 o'clock all well after a passage of 34 days. Just in time to write by Capt. Alexander who will sail tomorrow. I am too much engaged in receiving and arranging my goods to allow me to write a full letter. Mr. B.V.R. James has made provisions to bring my Brother from Niffau to this place and I believe has written you upon the subject.
>
> I am moving my effects into the mission house for the present but will be moved again up the River by the time my brother comes up. I expect as soon as I get my family made comfortably fixed to go in company with Brother James to select a suitable spot for the erection of the building of the Alexander High School. And Mr. Glasgow will commence immediately to make the brick. I expect as soon as I return to set about the building of my boat. Mr. Harrison is repairing his house for me. It will be done by the

time the boat is ready to take us up. You will please send out painters, oil, varnish and turpentine. It will save the building and save money in the end. My kindest regard to the members. [73]

Chapter 4
"We Did Well to Get Away Without Personal Injury"1863

Thomas has been waiting for advice from the Board for nearly four months about how to handle the increasingly dangerous circumstances of Niffau. A native man threatens to kill his wife Susanna, some natives are hostile toward the missionary family, and resources for the remote station are scarce. Within weeks of his January 5 letter, Thomas, Susanna and their daughters Emma and Georgianna are forced to flee. Natives drive them out of their house and steal their furniture and animals. Thomas relays the ominous circumstances to Lowrie whose response has been negligibly slow. He says:

> My Dear Sir, I deferred writing you for some months hoping that I should have received advice from you. But nothing has come to hand since I wrote you last September. The present state of our mission presents no very encouraging feature other than this--the natives are civil towards us generally though a few weeks since one came in our house with the intention to shoot my wife, as he said, though it was more to frighten than to kill. This, however, has been amicably settled.
>
> Our school is thinly attended and has been for some months past. I preach every Sabbath to as many as we can collect of the natives. But after all our exertion the number is small that hear the gospel. And of this small number I can only name two who have I think the least desire to [follow] through the word of God. John Peters, an old man, and Joseph--a boy that has been in our family for two years past, of whom I think I made mention in my last letter to you written from Greenville. I cannot say that the last year furnishes anything very encouraging to us as to any happy effect which the Gospel that we trust we have faithfully preached has had upon the minds of these

benighted heathen. Last October--the 25th I took a trip up through coast to Monrovia where I spent about 5 weeks among my friends on the Cape at Harrisburg, Mt. Coffee and Careysburg. By the change of the sea, food, company and scenery with some medical attention from Mr. B.V. R. James, my health is improved in some degree.

After two years [of] experience, my opinion is that it is not the best for a mission station to be in the midst of a native settlement like this. Certainly there is too much temptation to the natives to take advantage of the missionary by continually trespassing in one way or other. Besides, we can never have such control over the boys that may be in school as is necessary-- Not knowing what arrangements you have made for the present year for us and for our future procedure, I will leave this subject for the present.

I made my-- to Mr. James for [$]162 and --my balance for the said year. If you have not sent us an order for present year, you will please send by the earliest convenience--the order of goods and provisions which are inserted upon the order which accompanies this. If we continue this mission, trade goods and tobacco will be needed. If you have not already sent them you will please send the amount that you think we will need. Yours in the bonds of the gospel. [74]

By mid-January, writing from the safety of the Presbyterian Mission House in Monrovia, Thomas describes the circumstances that drove them and speculates about his future work.

We left Niffau on the 21st though not without considerable difficulty. We were obliged to leave the bell and doors. The natives stole a portion of our household furniture and took by force one goat & one fine sheep & a yearling calf. Many folks think we did well to get away without personal injury. At present we are pretty well and are looking forward with great anxiety to the time when we shall be settled in a field where our usefulness will be more apparent. My prayers have always been for divine direction.

> This I believe has been manifest, answered in the past and have no doubt will be in the future. My intention is to examine the country well before I decide as to the place of my future labors. I intend to visit Careysburg soon. There is doubtless a great work to be done among the settlers and I would like to situate myself so as to be able to devote a portion of my time there as well as to the heathen. The most of the people that have emigrated know very little of the great principles of our holy religion. And as we think the tenets of our church are the best in the world all being founded on the revealed word of God, we are desirous to see the word of God. We are desirous to see the borders of our Lion largely extended. I sent an order to you last month not knowing what would be our condition. Please do not send it. My Brother brought us out goods & provisions. He is now busily engaged building his boat and will soon have it ready for action. He is also making preparation for his school building, which I think will be the pattern Institution of Liberia. You will please send me a treatise on the principal branches of mathematics; one that will serve as a key to this system of knowledge. [75]

The *African Registry* publishes two detailed accounts between 1862 and 1863 about the Amoses' health and circumstances that cause them to abandon the Niffau mission. Thomas and James are eventually reassigned, changes that will acutely affect both their missionary careers and lives. The 1862 report states:

> The commencement of this station, situated half-way between Sinou and Cape Palmas was mentioned in the last Annual Report. At first, the attendance of the natives at religious service on the Sabbath was good, between two and three hundred being usually present. In January 1861, a boarding-school with twenty-four scholars was commenced. In March the school was reported as containing twenty scholars, and the aspect of the field still hopeful. In April, it was found to be very difficult to keep the boys in the school, the religious services were not well attended,

the head men were unwilling to protect the property of the mission, and no redress could be obtained for the articles stolen. In July, these brethren made a tour into the interior. They found the country very populous, the inhabitants kind to them, but most profoundly ignorant of divine things. It was their opinion, that for a hundred miles inland, if these tribes could be reached, the field of missionary labor would be far more encouraging than among the tribes of the coast.

On their return, they found their prospects still more discouraging and embarrassing. They describe the natives as outlaws, thieves and robbers-fraudulent, perfidious, and avaricious; and that even the traders cannot live among them, and seldom call at the settlement. Later accounts state that not a single headman was friendly to them or to their work, and that the children were all taken away from the school; that the health of Mr. James Amos had for months been suffering with fever, and the health of Mr. Thomas Amos was suffering also; that, in this state of things, they had come to the conclusion that it was best to suspend all further effort at the station for the space of two years. In these circumstances, the Committee authorized the return of Mr. James Amos, on the account of his health. They advised that a further trial be made of the mission under the charge of Mr. Thomas Amos, assisted by a competent teacher from Monrovia, one of the former scholars of the Alexander High School. [76]

The matter-of-fact August 1863 *African Repository* report blames "wicked and unfriendly" natives for the mission's failure.

The discouraging state of this station was mentioned in the last Annual Report. A further trial, however, was made to continue the missionary work among this wicked and unfriendly people. Mr. James R. Amos suffered so severely from fever that he was authorized to leave for the United States. His return to Africa and his employment there have been stated under the station at Harrisburgh [Harrisburg]. Left alone at Niffau, Mr. Thomas H. Amos

> tried most faithfully to sustain the station by continuing the school, preaching to the people, and visiting them and conversing with them separately. But every aspect of this work was discouraging. Few, and sometimes none, would attend preaching. The boys attended the school when they pleased, and would submit to no control. In the midst of these labours, the health of Mr. Amos suffered severely. In these circumstances it was decided to give up the station at least for the present. Mr. Amos will return to some place nearer Monrovia. There is abundant room and missionary work for him there. His station will be designated after hearing from himself and the brethren of the mission. [77]

Where the Presbyterian Board of Foreign Missions and American Colonization Society fall silent in exploring the root causes of difficulties missionaries like James and Thomas faced, historians readily elucidate. Exploring the rhetoric and realties of colonization, Tom W. Shick notes that "The motive behind the settlement of Afro-Americans in Liberia was destined to involve emigrants in conflicts as they struggled to maintain Western standards in the midst of a traditional African cultural environment." [78] The Amoses' letters reveal their firm belief in the supremacy of Euro-American religious doctrines. Their experiences, as described, also provide glimpses of the natives' lingering distrust of missionaries, Black and white, including those associated with the Ashmun Institute named to honor the man who massacred hundreds of Liberians.

Jehudi Ashmun's published history of Liberia vividly describes the violence he used to secure lands for settlers. Facing an army of 800 men sent to destroy his Monrovia settlement on November 11, 1822, the settler's fired their canons. He wrote:

> Imagination can scarcely figure to itself a throng of human beings in a more capital state of exposure to the destruc-

> tive power of the machinery of modern warfare! Eight hundred men here pressed shoulder to shoulder, in so compact a form that a child might easily walk upon their heads from one end of the mass to the other, presenting in their rear a breadth of rank equal to twenty or thirty men, and all exposed to a gun of great power, raised on a platform, at only thirty to sixty yards of distance! Every shot literally spent its force in a solid mass of living human flesh! Their fire suddenly terminated. A savage yell was raised, which filled the dismal forest with a momentary horror. [79]

The local chiefs' second assault on December 2 was crushed within less than two hours, according to Ashmun's account, evidence of God's providence. The enemy's losses evident from "the quantities of blood with which the field was found drenched," he said. [80] Shortly after the decisive fight, Ashmun, with the assistance of armed British soldiers, met with the chiefs whom they forced under gunpoint to cede land to the American settlers. The chiefs were "easily induced, but with affected resistance, to sign an instrument biding themselves to observe an unlimited truce with the colony" Ashmun said. [81] This second battle, according to Stebbins, was long "celebrated by the colonists with military parade, as the day on which they won a firm foothold on African soil; a terrible baptism of blood with which to consecrate a continent to Christian peace and love!" [82]

Ashmun, who used violence to repel attacks on the colony and the threat of violence to force local chiefs to give up portions of their lands to settlers, recorded an insightful observation that might have been useful to James and Thomas when they approached the ambivalent, often distrustful natives of Niffau. Ashmun said kings of some of the defeated (by battle or treaty) tribes regarded Black emigrants as "strangers who had forgot their attachment to the land of their fathers" and challenged them to renounce "their connexion with white men altogether and place themselves under the protection of the kings of the country." [8] The Niffau natives had viable concerns about emigrants and missionaries encroaching on their lands, customs and lifestyles.

Thomas and James's relationships with native people faltered partly because of their limited empathy. Nearly thirty years after the Ashmun-educated missionaries arrived in Liberia, Alexander Priestley Camphor, an African American missionary of the Methodist Episcopal Church, served there from 1896 to 1907. Camphor published *Missionary Story Sketches: Folk-lore from Africa,* a seminal work that provides insights into native Liberians beliefs and customs while keenly viewing, often critically, the influence of foreign missionaries and settlers on natives' lives. For example, he challenged European and American Christians to cease exporting rum to Liberia given its deleterious effect on the people whom missionaries purported to convert. He told them:

> "What white men make it for?" is the unanswerable query the poor heathen invariably makes as he comes to himself recovers his senses from his drunken stupor and revelries and sees the awful wreck made by rum upon his unfortunate brethren. Why, indeed, may we ask, do civilized nations send missionaries to the heathen in Africa, and in the same ship send tons of brutalizing and soul-destroying rum to sink the African to still lower depths of sin and shame? [84]

Camphor's collected stories show his intimate and personal contact with natives and are intended to engender sensitivity toward them as human beings in ways neither James nor Thomas seemed to accomplish. Instructed by their Board to learn the Kru language, James and Thomas made little progress. Camphor points out that missionaries used English language and literature in their evangelistic and educational work often to the disadvantage to their non-English speaking audiences. And native interpreters were not always able to convey the intended meanings of sermons or lessons. Hence, Camphor took time to learn some native languages and urged all missionaries to do the same. He demonstrated the effect of conveying religious themes in native language by publishing interpretations such as these:

" 'A muo klo be yu ti nyena

A neo naye so ba bla."

(We shall stand before the King.)

" ' Mma kwie n kboi Grepaw,

Mma kwie n kboi."

(Nearer my God, to Thee.) [85]

James and Thomas described native music and dance as offensive, complaining "Our ears are saturated almost daily with the sound of the war-horn and the furious yells of the naked savages."[86] Camphor explained native Liberians' fondness of dancing and singing within a cultural context.

> On moonlight nights they enjoy this into the late hours of the night. It is a common saying that when the moon is full all of Africa dances, and all night. The horn and drum are favorite musical instruments. To the ear of the stranger it is more noise than music, but by the native nothing better is desired. [87]

Similarly, Camphor described native religious rituals while explaining their spiritual meaning.

Religiously, the African is the child of some "charmed influence." To him the universe is controlled by spirit, and his creed is to be in perfect harmony with the world of spirits. He is ever alert to protect himself against the forces of evil about him. His faith rest in the fetish. Through its potency life may be prolonged, death vanquished, and miracles performed. Many mysterious demonstrations are performed by diviners, or sandmen, who are adepts in occult mysteries. They are dexterous in the making of characters in the sand, from which symbols they divine events. In this art the outside world knows but little what Africans claim to do. [88]

Summarizing native beliefs, James was more dismissive, saying "These people seem to be entirely ignorant of the existence of God. Their knowledge extends to that only which concerns their daily life."[89]

Camphor extolled the physical beauty of native Liberians in a manner rarely expressed by missionaries of the period.

The African natives, with their stalwart, athletic frames and iron constitutions, are noble specimens of physical manhood. And what possibilities there must be for a race for whom nature has done so much! The brawn and muscle of the African is his fortune. With these controlled by a cultivated and developed mind, he will rise in power and strength to the full accomplishment of his work and destiny on the continent. [90]

Keenly interested in learning names and their significance within the cultural context of Liberia, Camphor observed:

Names of native places and persons are not haphazardly given in Africa. Like names among the ancient Hebrews,

Alexander Priestley Camphor, missionary of Methodist Episcopal Church, and author of *Story Sketches: Folk-lore from Africa.*

> they are suggested by some physical act or idea. The native name of Monrovia, "Dru-Kau," the capital of Liberia, is derived from its nearness to an abundance of water… The native name of Careysburg, an inland Americo-Liberian town, is Fawblee. It means *bullock's rest.* The natives, with their caravans from the interior, traveling to the St. Paul's River and the settlement of the colonists, always rested at this spot with their burdens and bullocks; hence the names…African names are an interesting study and, always signifying thus something in native thought, have a force and beauty all their own. Missionaries, in changing children's names indiscriminately, destroy their tribes and homes. As a rule they ought not to be changed. Christian names may be easily added to the native name. [91]

While James and Thomas were clearly committed to educating children whom they described as the heart of their mission, their letters seldom refer to those children by name. The few who are mentioned have Anglicized names and are praised for their "civilized" conduct and willingness to embrace Christianity.

Chapter 5
"This is My Resignation from All Connection with the Presbyterian Board of Foreign Missions"
1863-1864

"I have one hundred bricks to make, and to put up the builings when they are made," Samuel Glasgow tells his brother, praising the building trend in Liberia that favors his brickmaking business. "There will be more than fifty new brick buildings go[ing] up on the St. Paul's river this season." [92] Like his earlier letter, this one extols the growth conditions of the colony and progress of Ashmun's missionaries. Reprinted in the *African Repository,* Glasgow's emotive first-hand account of his experience as an emigrant is akin to a testimony, evidence of the divinely sanctioned mission of colonization. He tells his yet to be convinced to emigrate brother that Liberia's prestige is growing; he and fellow emigrants are blessed materially and spiritually in ways not possible in the United States. He says:

> Liberia is on the upward. I believe that God is in the work. If my son Samuel was here, as good a workman as he is, he could make a first rate living, setting and burning bricks alone.--a Dutch man-of-war came into the port of Monrovia and saluted our flag which was returned. We have entered into commercial treaties with several Powers, this showing that Liberia ranks with the nations of the world. Our legislature adjourned on last Thursday after a session of six weeks. I exhibited a coffee huller to the members, and have applied for a patent for it. It is my own invention. I have sent to Baltimore my patterns to have castings made to the extent of several hundred dollars' worth. Dear brother, I thank God for his goodness to me. I left my home yesterday morning at sunrise, and before the sun set today I made thirteen dollars with my own hands. Rev. James R. Amos and family are all well. The two young

> men that came out with him have both had the fever, and are about again. They are pleased with their new homes. [93]

Like Samuel, James is optimistic about his role in Liberia's progress. Now stationed in Harrisburg and his brother Thomas and family safely ensconced for the time being at the Presbyterian mission house in nearby Monrovia, James is reenergized and busily organizing the construction project. He envisages Alexander High School one day rivaling Liberia College, the country's leading higher education institution, and intends to lead the school in that direction. He offers to purchase books to stock the library if necessary and recommends Thomas for a professorship at the school. Other details discussed include his construction of a river boat that affords him much needed mobility, supply purchases, and Glasgow's progress in making the bricks.

> My press of work gives me but very little time to write. Brother Thomas with his family has arrived safe from Niffau. He is much in need of a few months rest. There is a good deal of interest manifested concerning the Alexander High School and I have had several application[s] for admission of students. This school will doubtless rival the Liberia College if it is rightly managed, which, so far as breath in me by Divine guidance, I shall endeavor to do. There are some young men here who desire to study theology, a department which will be necessary to connect with the Alexander High School. The hope of our church in this country will depend for its ministers and teachers in a great measure upon this school. And if I think that my brother could not be better employed than to have a professorship in this school so that we may be able to give those young men who are looking forward to the work of the ministry a liberal knowledge of the doctrines of the gospels which seems to be very little understood by the present incumbents of the Presbyterian pulpits in this country. I speak not disrespectful[ly]. My boat is nearly completed and I think that I am not exaggerating by say-

> ing that it will be the greatest achievement ever made in boat building in Liberia. Mr. Glasgow is making the brick for the building. He furnishes everything but wood and sand boards for wheeling on and the tables and makes sets and--them good quality for 3 dollars per thousand. Mr. James will write you concerning the land, the deed for which he gets for you in fee simple. I have engaged the shingles 5 inches broad common length at 9 dollars per thousand. Mr. Simon Harrison has done up the house of which I spoke very nicely and I expect to move into it in a few days. [94]

A consummate scholar, James next turns an attentive eye to the quality of instructional materials, noting the immediate need to restock and upgrade.

> I have examined the library and apparatus of the Alexander High School. I find the former what remains very badly mutilated. The school books have been for the most part spirited away. In my next I will give you an exact account of the number of volumes in the library. The philosophical apparatus is in tolerable good order. Also the astronomical with the exception of the axes of the earth which is out of repair. The electric machine is entirely out of order. [95]

Stating "the necessity of asking" for updated books, James's order includes English grammar, "Davies Algebra or any classical or scientifical works which are essential," "Spencer's Arnold first and second Latin," "Greek and Latin testaments," "Elements of Mineralogy," "Brocklesby's Elements of Meteorology," "Whitlocks Geometry and Surveying," and "1 copy of Hebrew and English pronouncing Bible." [96] He adds, "Those books which I have ordered I must have and if they cannot be given to the school I will pay for them and charge the students." The attached addendum lists food rations including flour, meal, sauerkraut, mackerel, pork, herring, ham, cheese, crushed sugar, tea and domestic items such as table clothes, dress patterns and a flour sieve. [97]

But James becomes increasingly frustrated when the requested items and supplies do not arrive on schedule. He asserts that the Board's disconnect from on-the-ground circumstances like weather and building and labor costs could undermine the construction project. His April and May letters foreshadow difficulties. Exasperated, he tries to clarify his Baltimore expenditures to Lowrie.

> Yours of the 11th of December/62 came to hand today. I cannot account for the detention. I am very sorry that my last before leaving Baltimore was not understood satisfactorily. I thought that I had given the different bills as distinctly as possible. I do not know how the difference between Dr. Hall's bill and mine occurs. I think however that my bill is correct. I bought precisely according to our arrangement made when I was in New York. I could not give all the items because my own two hundred dollars were spent permissively among yours and I report a correct account of the different amounts but not the small articles. The amount therefore stands as follows: 50 dollars for carpenter tools; 50 dollars for housing goods; 54 dollars for boast; 229 dollars for tobacco; and 213 dollars for provisions and dry goods. And for my brother's supplies 189 dollars $776.00, $442.00 is being expended for building purposes and contingent expenses. My own supplies is on the account of my private $200 dollars. I have already ordered my next supplies which I hope you will have sent out when this reaches you. My boat cost about 50 dollars expenses beside my own labor. She is the finest boat on the St. Paul's River and will amply pay for herself. She is 35 feet long and 7 feet beam. She is propelled by 2 side wheels like a steam boat, only requires the same number of boys as an oar boat. She has a forward deck sufficient to transport goods dry in the midst of the rain. If I had had such a one at Niffau it might [have] saved us some $400 dollars. I have not made as much progress with the build-

> ing as I expected in the same time. But for Africa I suppose it is fast work, at least it is thought so. [98]

Next, he discusses progress with the brick making and costs of cultivating land purchased surrounding the school site, and the need for specific building supplies.

> Mr. Glasgow has the brick nearly ready to burn. The kiln is set and he is putting up the casing today. I have been moved to Harrisburg about one month. I have cleared and burnt off about eight acres of the land and expect in a few days to plant it in rice, potatoes, cassads [cassavas] and other vegetables. If you would have the whole 55 acres planted down in coffee, in four years from the date of planting it would yield sufficient annually to supply every member of the board in coffee. 50 acres 300 trees per acre=15,000 trees 6 pounds per tree=90,000 pounds. It cost about five dollars per acre to clear the land---There was nothing said about nails, paints, hinges and sockets, etc. But I suppose that you will send them out. Also a piazza around those brick walls will be essential to their preservation as paint to the wood work. Of this I wish your advice...If you will be so kind as to send me a can of varnish I can make the most of the furniture that I will require which will be economy [economical]... I am getting lumber-- ready according to your directions. But I think now as the appearance of the showers seems to indicate early raining season that I had not best commence raising the brick wall till after the rains for fear we spoil our good job. But have everything ready so that we can put it up immediately after the rains and we will have a good permanent building. All that we will lose by the detention will be a few months loss time. And on the other hand [what] we will gain perhaps is the value of the building by putting everything up dry. I expect to have the brick carried to the place of building and a temporary shed put over them. The sand delivered and also the lumber all prepared, etc. [99]

What James next announces shows his self-directed decision making, a trait that puts him at odds with the paternalistic Board. He has convened classes of the yet to be completed Alexander High School in his home. Justifying this action, he says:

> The urgency of idle students compelled me to open the first session of the Alexander High School in 1863 in my private house. I have therefore opened on the first day of April with 3 young men, two of whom have been taken under the care of the Presbytery of W. Africa and are pursuing their studies with the view of the holy ministry. There will be more students invited to the school as soon as I can procure for them boarding places in the neighborhood. The Alexander High School is looked upon by our church and by many citizens with a great deal of interest. Nearly all the young men that have been educated in Liberia received their education in the Alexander High School. It evidently has been the greatest success in educational point of any others in this republic. As the venerable Dr. Alexander has immortalized himself in the United States, so will his name live in Africa. And I hope to see the day when this institution shall be called the Alexander University and Theological Seminary. [100]

"I am quite impatient for the material that you are to send out for the building," he writes to a still unresponsive Lowrie in early May. "I cannot proceed much further without it. I am however in good hopes that it will come in time to complete the building this year." [101] Undeterred, he explains costs, weather conditions and his efforts to ensure that the project proceeds as planned.

> I am still going on perseveringly to get everything else ready. The bricks are now ready for going into the wall. The boards for the floors are all jointed and piled. The sheeting and other lumber is being got. I cannot commence the walls until I get the frames. I have made and burned in good order 88,000 bricks. The cost of making is $3.50 per--and cost $308. The cost of digging well to

water the clay $7, making $315. And to Mr. Melville for delivering 23 cord [boards] of wood--the sand for making the brick, making the floors, shedding and board for tables 4128. For 5000 feet of boards at $35 per thousand $175. I have paid about $75 dollars on other lumber but as I have not the contract completed I cannot give you exact account. The lime I shall not purchase till I am ready to put the walls up as it must not lay on sands in the rains. The sand also cannot be delivered without taking damage or being wasted by those washing rains. Therefore I can do but little more than the carpenter work till the rains are over. I have put shed over the brick to keep them from the heavy rains. I have the lumber also secured from the weather. You will please give me instructions in reference to a piazza around the building which by all means ought to be done to save the building. I have thought to attach the kitchen to the main building in order to save one wall, one story high fourteen feet by twelve. I shall depend on you to send nails--hinges, catches, locks, fastenings, paints and please send me 1 can of white varnish so that I may make my own furniture.

The mission of this place is still lingering. There is no school at all. Uncle Simon's boys seem to take more interest and seem willing to heed discipline better than formerly. Uncle Simon himself does all that he can. I am sorry to learn that you are much pressed for funds. If the Lord is for us, who can prevail against us. Pray for us. [102]

The Board faces myriad challenges to supporting its mission stations in Liberia. Deliveries of food and household supplies are delayed and often insufficient. At times, the Board's communication is unresponsive to James and Thomas's requests for specific instructions. The latter is evident in James's two July letters to Walter Lowrie whose delayed (or detained) responses fuel his frustration.

James's July 1 letter devotes detailed effort to address

Board questions about his Baltimore expenditures for the building as well as food items and other expenses. Having apparently received a delayed April response from Lowrie, he notes:

> In a letter enclosed in the same envelope within this you will find a rejoinder to the first of your letter dated April 9th. The next is in reference to my purchases in Baltimore. In a former letter I have given you the account of these purchases which you have received long ere this--as it is possible that it didn't reach you. I will send you the duplicate. Just at this moment a note is handed me from Mr. [B.V.R.] James in which he states that you have requested him to ask me concerning these purchases in Baltimore and write you in return mail. Now my dear sir. I would prefer Mr. James, my other dear friend in Liberia, to do business for me if I were unable to attend to it myself or to act for me counsel where the third person is required. But I hope that you will allow me to attend to my part of the business which simply concerns you and me. I thought when I began this letter that I could give you the duplicate of my letter of April-- But as it has got mislaid somehow in moving, I cannot put my hands on it. I therefore will give it to you as nearly as I can.
>
> Purchases as follows--$50; boat apparatus $54. Housing goods $50; Fish and butter; tobacco $229.60. Dry goods 4115. Meat and flour $58. Amount $596.60. My brother's bill $150= 776.60. Over this bill I bought $200 worth for which I spent my private funds. This amount was for my own provisions. The $596.60 was for the mission. As there was nothing said about provisions for myself when I saw you, I thought there would be no difficulty about it. For at that time all these things that I have given you the account of were designated for the mission. I think that if you had not let this slip your memory there would have been no difficulty.
>
> You speak of Dr. Hall presenting a small cash bill of $35. But this is not a separate bill from the above. Dr. Hall gave me $35 but I had paid the same out of my funds for part of

the materials for the boat. And it is included in the $596.60. If he has charged it as a separate account it is a palpable mistake. When I settled with Dr. Hall the account stood correct with the above. I sent you the precise account of all with the exception of the freight on my $300 which did not, I think, fill more or but little more space than was allowed once on the ship. You will remember that I did not make all my purchases in Baltimore. The tools and several other articles were bought in Philadelphia. I found that I could buy them cheaper and better quality than I could obtain them in Baltimore. I paid for the things in Philadelphia out of my own fund and in Baltimore I took the same amount of your money to pay for my own provisions. I did this for economy's sake which all amounts to the same thing at last.

However to make it still more plain I will give you the whole as follows. $596.60; for the mission + $180.00; for my brother+$200.00; for myself=$976.60-$200.00=$776.60-$180=$596.60=the bill of goods purchased in Baltimore for the mission; and must be charged to it. The freight on my bill $200 I left as mentioned above, but if you think that is not right, you must charge it to my account. I hope that this account will be understood satisfactional [satisfactory].

I am making every exertion to get all the materials together for the building so as to put it up as soon as the rains will admit. The sash and hardware have not yet arrived. We are looking for the *Stevens* any day. I have not yet received your letter but have answered the duplicate or copy. It is the letter by ship which I [have] not received. We have selected a beautiful site for the building. Nearly all the settlements from Muhlenberg Mission to White Plains and Millsburg Missions a distance of 9 miles in equilateral triangle.

The risers for the first flight of stairs in the Alexander High School building are rosewood. The cost is the same as other lumber. The first floor African poplar. 2nd and 3rd floors

> are persimmon. Please give direction concerning piazza. By all means it should envelope the whole house. Please direct for fencing out building. I have planted vegetables and rice on the mission ground so as not to lose the land that had to be cleared to get a site for the building. [103]

Within several days James receives an adamant response from Lowrie scolding him for incorrectly assuming that he is the appointed principal of Alexander High School. James understood this to be the case and is astonished and offended that the Board would do otherwise. His July 8 remarks to Lowrie are direct.

> Yours of the 29th of April I have received. You say you are greatly surprised to find by my communication of February 3rd that I considered myself principal of the Alexander School. I can only say in reply that while I knew that there was no formal appointment yet the impression was made by your own communications not only upon myself, but also upon Mr. James and also my brother.

> If you meant by stating the Alexander High School was committed to my charge simply that the erection of the building of the Alexander High School was committed to my charge, and that the library and apparatus was in my care for safe keeping, it was construed [as] an informal appointment of me as principal. I assure you my dear sir that I do not presume to usurp such a responsible office as this. I am sorry that the impression was made. Yet I am glad that it was but an impression. I feel that to be appointed principal of that school is to be appointed to the highest office or position in the Liberian Mission. I do not feel adequate to the task. And I am quite relieved on reading your statement, though I think it is a harsh correction of such an important mistake. I hope that hereafter we shall understand each other more correctly.

> I think that I have no disposition to arrogate to myself more than what justly belongs to me. I had not the most remote idea when I proposed this building that it would

> be the Alexander High School building but the Harrisburg Mission. But when you wrote me just before I left the States that the building was for the Alexander High School and the mission remaining as it had been, and the communications expressly stating that my mission was connected with the said Alexander High School and no one else appointed for it, it was accepted as an informal appointment to that charge. The letter I sent you dated February 3rd was handed to Mr. James and also to my brother to read before [it] went to mail. And they both evidently were under the same impression that I was or they would not have approved of it. I only make these statements to show that I do not wish to take improper steps to come into notoriety. For I have been always promoted faster than I have deserved without undue effort on my part. I hope therefore that you will forgive any seeming impertinence written you by me touching this matter. It is a lesson from which I have been greatly profited. [104]

In late August James answers another Board letter questioning building costs. While doing so he asserts his previous experience as a building superintendent at Ashmun Institute and reminds the Board of its' limited understanding of labor and costs of clearing a Liberian forest in order to construct the school building. The underlying and ultimately insurmountable issue for James, however, is the Board's reduction of his missionary work to a "mechanical trade." Again, his remarks to Lowrie are direct.

> Yours of the 24 of June came to hand today. As I have written you on the subject contained in the first of your letter I shall therefore in my reply commence at your fourth proposition.
>
> 4th You say "We did not contemplate clearing off and land. This is very much like your want of contemplating the great expense of this building." In the name of common sense, how could you expect me or anyone else to know

the spot to put the building in an impenetrable forest without cutting the bush? If I had erected the building in an unstable place it would have been an irreparable mistake which would have been regretted. I assure you sir that I have had to clear off nearly as much more. And I feel assured that if you were here you would be pleased with the course that I have taken.

5th You say "We were greatly surprised to learn that you had opened the Alexander High School." To this I have written in a former letter and will only say now that I am quite as much surprised to learn that my missionary work has dwindled into a mechanical trade or builder. If this were only a dream my wandering spirit would soon return to its ---tabernacle and awake and rejoice that it was but a dream.

6th You say that you do not know what I mean and I mean to say that for the protection of the walls and for the convenience of the building there ought to be a two story piazza on each side if not entirely around the building.

7th Relates to my supplies.

8th "If it be absolutely necessary you may draw on Mr. James for $200." Now I presume that you have very limited conception of the expense of this building. You cannot judge their building from the calculation that I gave you in New York, for the building that I had in contemplation was a private house like Mr. Miller's. And even in that I only gave the calculation for making and laying the brick. Experience is the best calculation in Africa. Your direction for this building makes it quite a costly building. 43 feet long by 22 feet.

I superintended the building of the Ashmun Institute which was only 8 feet longer and 18 feet wider at a cost of nearly $1,000 finished in the plainest style where everything is convenient to obtain. But only think of this place where there is nothing convenient and where everything has to be carried on the heads of natives--from 14 to 4 miles. This building might have been erected for nearly one thousand dollars less on the Cape. The foundation stone [s] are to be carried about 7 miles, the brick nearly the same. Lumber from 1 to 14 miles. This building cannot be completed with less than three thousand dollars. I will not be circumscribed to $200 nor $300 in drafts. If you expect me to finish the building you must allow me to draw on Mr. James for as much as it will require to do it. So far as I am concerned I will try finishing it as judicious[ly] as I can and for the lowest cost possible. But to be confined to such a small inadequate amount I will not. If I am not to draw the money at the time needed and the amount required as it is needed, please give me an honorable discharge from my superintendence of the building. Only one of these two things can be done. The last tobacco sent out is of such an inferior quality that I fear Mr. James will not be able to get the cost out of it. I can hardly get any of it off my hands here in Harrisburg.

9th "Please write fully, etc" The following is the list of the items already contracted and paid for. The making and burning of 88,000 brick @3.50/100=$3,08. Well @$7=315. Mr. Melville's bill for wood and sand, etc $128. For cutting bush $30. 5000 feet of boards @ 4 & 3 ½ $175. To Simon Harrison for [joints] and timber $68. Shed over carpenter work $100. Cutting roads and bridges for carrying material $25. For moving up $50. For making boat $50. For boat in Baltimore $54. For tools $50. For dozen goods $50. For boarding work men $50.

Therefore out of the five hundred and ninety six obtained in Baltimore together with $250 in drafts I returned goods--for the amount $1162.00 besides the hiring of my boat hand which I have charged to my account. At the very best calculation $2000 more, including the tobacco just received will be required. Had this been good tobacco it would have nearly accomplished it. I am very sorry that Dr. Hall made such an important mistake in collecting it. As you may not understand what has been said about roads and bridges for $25, I will explain. I pay for cutting foot paths

> for carrying materials at the rate of $3 for 20 chains. I have had to cut in different paths for the about 135 chains over five creeks. I had to make foot bridges, all of which have cost $25. [105]

In spite of delays in the delivery of supplies, damage to his boat, and seasonal rains, James continues working. He reflects on Lowrie's letters, calling his mode of scolding "uncourteous and unchristian." He feels undervalued and disrespected. Once he completes the building he intends to resign from the Presbyterian Board of Foreign Missions and return to the United States.

> Yours of the 22nd and 31st of Aug. are at hand. The vessel bringing the doors, sash and hardware has arrived safely. I am very sorry that you did not send according to promise the balance of my order, and the order which I sent for provisions to assist in boarding the workmen at the building. The rains have passed over and I have recommenced the building in earnest, and making as much progress as possible. I think that the roof will be on by the first of March. The high waters [have] done considerable damage to my boat. I had her anchored in Mr. Melville's dock bank where I thought she would be perfectly safe; but one night the waters rushed out with such fury that it caused her to drag out into the river. She then started down the rapids and the anchor caught in the rock and parted. She capsized breaking all her machinery, and went down the rapid current about 10 miles before she could be brought to the shore. Her hull is uninjured.
>
> Whatever judgment you will pass upon the following I know not. But I feel it to be my duty to write though it is very painful thing to write. After much deep thought and earnest prayer upon the subject I have come to the conclusion, deliberately but positively, to withdraw from the field of labor which I now occupy and from my present relation to your Board, and therefore this is my resignation from all connection with the Presbyterian Board of Foreign Missions to take place on the first day of May 1864,

Lord willing, which will allow you ample time to fill the vacancy.

My reasons for resigning from the Board are as follows:

1st I have been deceived in the intensions of the Board which has resulted in my injury. When I visited you last year I requested you to grant me the control of the Harrisburg Mission. The reasons which I gave you for making this request were 1st That Simon Harrison's Mission was a nuisance and a great disappointment. 2nd That his labors were not acceptable to the people. 3rd That it was the people's request that I should be sent to them. And 4th that God had abundantly blessed my labors while I was among them.

2nd As I entirely misunderstood the relation which I sustained to the Alex. High School and it was circulated abroad by inferences drawn from your own writings that the said school was in my charge; I therefore regard the manner by which you corrected that mistake as being altogether uncourteous and unchristian. And again your erroneous publication in the Report of May 1863 relative to Simon Harrison being a licentiate and supplying the Harrisburg Church is not true for Mr. Harrison never was acknowledged as a licentiate by our presbytery and therefore is not and cannot be a supply for that pulpit.

And 3rd that "Mr. Amos is preaching in the neighborhood" is equally untrue for I have been supplying the Harrisburg church since February.

4th Your communication of June 24th in the latter part of the 5th proposition. You say "After the building is finished there will be plenty of spheres of usefulness for you in Liberia. I cannot but feel somewhat chafe at this remark!

All of the above I regard as good reasons for the dissolution of my connection with the Board. --- good and sufficient reasons why you should accept my resignation. I expect, Lord willing, to return to the States. I feel assured

> that you will bear part of my expenses. Therefore in all good conscience toward the P.B. of F Missions I entertain no ill feeling, but believe and accept it as the order of an All wise but mysterious providence and though incomprehensible yet shall result in good. And He who ordereth all events shall be glorified therefore. With humble resignation I am yours most sincerely. [106]

Four months later, James's final letter announces a startling misfortune: the roof of the completed Alexander High School has collapsed. Although repairable, the Board will have to invest even more funds in the long-awaited building. Scheduled to sail to the United States in May, James posits the hand of God is involved.

> It is no uncommon thing for the most sanguine expectations of men to be blighted. The fluctuations of prosperity and its opposite adversity are only to remind us of the great truth. That in each event of life the hand of an overruling providence is manifested. It is with pain and the deepest regret that I have to inform you of a very unexpected disaster which happened to the building. After having nearly completed the roof the workmen were just finishing the cast shingling when an accidental separation of the upper girder took place and the weight of the roof drove out the two side walls breaking them about the upper window seats and leaving the--two sides of the upper story and the roof in ruins. I think that no blame can be attached to any of the workmen or to myself. Although a thousand different--might now be suggested, any of which would have prevented accident. But no one I think who had never seen of known of a building falling in the same way would have thought that these girders were not sufficiently fastened. The loss sustained I think is about three hundred dollars. Very little of the wood work is impaired...Rafters are uninjured. Very little if anything entirely destroyed, except some of the brick. I will give you the estimate of cost on the account of building. The car-

> penter work was nearly all done, floors ready to go down. Stairway stuff was made. Casings and everything all to putting up--plastering. $300 dollars more would have completed the building. I thought best for the good of the mission that Mr. Melville finish the building for reasons which I will state to you when I see you personally. As I feel that my mission work for the present is done in Liberia. I shall, Lord willing, sail for the United States about the first of May. [107]

Upon resigning, James asks the Board for $500 to cover his return trip home; an expense usually covered. James departs Liberia between May and July of 1864. He resumes working as pastor of First Colored Presbyterian Church in Reading, PA. According to Joseph H. Wilson's *Presbyterian Historical Almanac and Annual Remembrancer of the Church,* James was "anxious to become a useful citizen" and "few men have shown greater zeal, or more determined perseverance in that direction." [108] James dies on November 17, 1864 of hectic fever (consumption). Ashmun alumni honor him by passing a series of resolutions, including the following: "*Resolved,* That we will imitate his example by our untiring efforts for the dissemination of religion, literature, and the principles of true morality among our race." [109]

Chapter 6
"We Need Not Expect to Get Good Health in This Country"1863-1869

James had worked as an itinerant minister before enrolling at Ashmun and embarking on a career as a missionary in Liberia where he held temporary assignments between 1859 and 1864. Thomas's tenure in Liberia from 1859 to 1869, though longer, consists of short-term pastor assignments in Marshall and Monrovia, and as a financial agent for the Presbyterian Board of Foreign Missions.

By April 1863 Thomas has recovered from the Niffau debacle and searches settler communities for his next job. Discovering the need for a church within the mostly Americo-Liberian community of Marshall, a port city about 45 miles south of Monrovia, he organizes a congregation and proposes to lead it. A defining shift in interest, he now prefers ministering to settlers rather than "heathen" natives. He and Susanna experience recurring illness during his brief work in Marshall and request to visit the United States for "the benefit of health." However, Susanna's health worsens and she dies before they can leave.

During a yearlong furlough from 1864 to 1865, Thomas and his children reside in Philadelphia and Reading, PA, where he serves as an occasional preacher at First Colored Presbyterian, his brother's former church. He remarries and soon accepts the invitation from B.V.R. James and the First Presbyterian Church of Monrovia congregation to serve as pastor. Like the Marshall church, the Monrovia congregants are mostly Americo-Liberians. In May 1866 fellow Presbyterian minister E.W. Blyden, who later becomes a leading Pan-Africanist scholar promoting Islam over

Christianity, preaches the sermon at Thomas's installation. Within this settler church Blyden agitates against elitism and colorism, an action Thomas believes undermines his influence as pastor. Active in the social life of Monrovia, Thomas co-founds the Masonic Grand Lodge and serves as Deputy Grand Master until his death.

Throughout his ten years in Liberia, Thomas devotes his efforts to building stable churches by improving physical structures and through evangelism and weekly prayer meetings. He is equally committed to ensuring that settlers and natives who take an interest receive a formal, English education, and urges improving the quality of the Alexander High School teachers. Much to his increasing disillusionment and dismay, the Presbyterian Board of Foreign Missions consistently underfunds churches and education. Still, Thomas remains devoted to the emigration cause. Writing to former teacher and mentor John Miller Dickey, Thomas urges him to continue encouraging Blacks to emigrate to Liberia where they have the best opportunity for civil and political rights. After another bout of illness, Thomas dies in July 1869, leaving a mortgage on a house that he has painstaking built with limited income and resources. Within months of his death as fellow ministers and masons extol his religious and civic legacy, Thomas's widow Sarah and children, including three-year old Thomas Hunter Amos who will eventually attend Lincoln University, prepare to leave Liberia.

***

As James works to complete the Alexander High School, Thomas explores settler and native communities where he might start a new mission. Still waiting to hear if the Board will assign him to assist his brother in Harrisburg, he visits Careysburg at the urging of his erstwhile classmate Armistead Miller who established a Presbyterian mission and school in Mount Coffee. Named to honor Lott Cary, one of the first Black American Baptist missionaries who helped Jehudi Ashmun defend the colony against native Africans, the community is located about 30 miles south of Mt. Coffee. Thomas visits Careysburg twice and preaches by invitation at the Methodist and Baptist congregations. Although Presbyterians living in the area have yet to organize a church, Thomas decides there was not a sufficient following to warrant a new mission.

By April of 1863, he turns his attention to the Marshall settlement which has about 100 Americo-Liberian inhabitants and 100 recaptives; an ideal place for a new Presbyterian church. His overview of the mission's potential is enthusiastic. He says:

> Sunday the 19th day of April I organized a church here of 20 members. Fourteen are communicants. I baptized six recaptives on the confession of their faith in Christ. I have great reason to hope they are in a [regenerated] state. Four others presented themselves for baptism but I thought best to advise them to wait until I shall return to that place, which I hope to do next week. These boys, Congos, promised me faithfully, that they will not cease praying to Jesus until they shall find him to be indeed their Savior. We have great reason to rejoice over the blessed work that is going on among the recaptives in Marshall which I consider we may attribute to the pious efforts of their guardians. These above mentioned are in the hands of our members, persons of respectability and piety. I am not building here on another man's foundation, but I can rejoice that the blessing of God was upon my labor in this place the few days I was there. This field has been neglected very much. The Methodists and Baptists each have a church in Marshall, but they are supplied with ministers quite unqualified for

> their task. I found the people much like sheep having no shepherd. [110]

Next, he reports the details of an extensive exploration he and colleagues make of inland native territories where future missions might be established.

> Three beautiful rivers conjoin at Marshall which gives easy access to a large portion of the country, both in Montasarrado County and Grand Bassa County. Junk River, Farmington and Little Bassa Rivers. The first towns I visited are on or near the Farmington River which runs due east from the sea, navigable about 15 miles. King Jimy's town is about 8 miles from Marshall. Here we gave some religious instruction after introducing ourselves as missionaries and explaining our wish to visit then often and preach to them the word of God. They treated us kindly and bid us come again. We again took our canoe and went about 6 miles further where we came to another town, though not quite so large as the first, it being of about 100 inhabitants. Here too we conversed upon the subject of religion. We found them ready and willing to hear the work of God.
>
> There are three other towns in the neighborhood of this and much larger. But E.W. Wright thought best we should return to Marshall. To this I cheerfully consented being weary. Therefore we did not visit them. Two days after we visited two towns which are situated near the Little Bassa River. The first place we stopped was at [Summertroys] Town about 6 miles from Marshall and about 2 miles north of the Little Bassa River at the head of a--navigable for a canoe, subject to the tide. Here we were kindly received and spent an hour or more in conversation with the king, a man of considerable wit--useful instruction and general improvement among his people. He promises to prepare a house for the worship of God if I will come and preach for them occasionally.
>
> Leaving this place we went about 8 miles further and came to the [Kidoielar's] Town. [Possibly Kuno Kree's Town ac-

> cording to 1850 and 1870 maps]. Here we stayed all night. The people were hospitable and mannerly. Here we gave religious instruction to a good number. The natives generally through this country are more civilized than the Kroo natives and treat the Americans with more friendship and show signs of greater preparation to hear the gospel. These towns are about 100 to 150 inhabitants each and call strongly for a missionary to come and labor among them. A mission with a good canoe may reach these and many more towns from Marshall and may therefore through God's grace do a good work among the settlers, the recaptives and the natives of the country. If you have not selected a field for me, why not enter into this and I know of men where I can hope to be more useful. [111]

Concluding, he informs Lowrie and the Board: "Should you desire that my future labor shall be in this field I shall require you to help us build a church. The people are poor, though willing to do all they can in the way of giving labor and there is a steam saw mill at this place and lumber can be easily obtained at the usual process." [112] He also requires a permanent house and canoe.

> I shall need a house for my dwelling. If you will furnish me $300, I will manage to build a house on my own lot in that place. I think as my health is feeble it is no more than right that I should have a shelter for my family that they can call their own and I am sure you will not think my request unreasonable. I shall need a canoe sufficiently large to carry my family and capable of going to sea. This will cost not less than $50. [113]

Thomas's June and September letters detail his efforts to support the growing mission church in Marshall, including a testimony of a recently converted recaptive woman named Martha, and a request for free medicines. While Board resources have declined due to revenue losses during the Civil War, Thomas continues working to build the Marshall mission that he hopes will include a school. He secures a lot from the government on which to build a church and purchases a temporary house with his own money. He continues to struggle with poor health.

On June 2, he reports:

I have just returned from Marshall, the place of which I spoke in my last dated April--Our church is in a flourishing state. Sabbath, May 17th I administered the sacraments of the Lord's Supper. It was truly a season of refreshing to us, 16 communed. We did not admit our recaptive members to the table this time, deeming it advisable for them to be better instructed as to the nature and utility of this most hopeful ordinance than it has been in our power to do in so short a time. We are quite hopeful, however, that they will be prepared against our next communion season. We have now 7 recaptives baptized members and 2 natives of the Bassa country, 9 in all. We have great reason to hope that these have experienced a change of heart. We have repeatedly noticed them seeking places of solitude for devotion. I do most heartily rejoice that my Divine Master hath permitted me to see this number though small it be of Afric's heathen sons mourning at the foot of the cross of our dear Lord and earnestly crying for his rich mercies. Truly Christ is exalted to give repentance for, as well, as remission of sins.

A few days since Rev. E.W. Wright, Elder of our church--with 7 recaptives started from home for his farm--is about 9 miles from Marshall in canoes, the tide waters coming in very strong which caused considerable agitation in the river. The canoe filled with water and there appeared for some minutes no alternative but that some if not all must be lost. But what is most worthy of notice is this: that while all the recaptives except one, Martha, were crying the one to the other for help Martha called most faithfully upon the Lord Jesus to save her soul, acknowledging at the same time her utter unworthiness. Martha is one of the recaptive members of our church. The canoe did not go down and none were lost. Natives in such extremities are likely to call upon wither their living or dead relatives for help. But Martha is unwilling to trust any other friend than Christ and his merit alone.

Our meetings in the settlement have been well attended both by the recaptives and the settlers. I did not visit the native settlements this time, the weather being quite unfavorable. I am now very anxious to hear from you and your conclusions in regard to my new field of labor. I suppose your funds are not plus at this time. I hear you have suffered a heavy loss this year. This is a providence beyond your control. God will doubtless take care of his own work. He will not suffer his work to cease for want of means to carry it on, though he calls sometime upon his servants to undergo privations for his own namesake that he may prove them. But they may rejoice in this. He will not leave them or forsake them.

My health is not very good, though it is better I think than it was some time since. Should you conclude to sustain the mission at Marshall I shall be glad to commence the building--and to move my family at once. It is no advantage to live on the Cape any longer since my work is not here. My Bro. James and family are pretty well. [114]

The Board's delayed response to Thomas's letters during this period may be due to interruptions caused by the war. Some correspondence had to be sent by way of England. Undaunted, he continues addressing the needs in Marshall. His June 8 letter reveals that he is acting as a doctor and requires medicines for the station.

I wrote you by Capt Yates in April & by way of England the latter part of May---In there I explained to you all the particulars relative to my proceedings since we left Niffau. I suppose these letters have been received seasonable. Now having this favorable opportunity, I send a small or-

> der which if [you] will fill & forward to us this fall you will do a great kindness. I wrote you in February last, countermanding my order previously sent in--consequence of the supplies brought to us by Rev. James. In sending this, I take for granted that the others have been destroyed, or at least will not be filled. The medicines I have ordered I shall need if you station me at Marshall. There is no doctor there and I shall be compelled to practice medicine more or less, as it is generally thought that this is part of the missionary work. Of course I shall get no pay & I hope therefore that you will not charge the medicine to my account except you are compelled to do so. If so, you will please to make the bill very small. This order of supplies had better be sent to Marshall if you order me to go there before the things come to this coast. We are all pretty well at present. [115]

Commuting between Monrovia and Marshall, Thomas
102 hopes to establish mission school there. His September update explains the expenses he incurs for the mission. He provides more specific details about his health challenges.

> Our little church at Marshall is still encouraging. I have not been there for some weeks. I intend going there as soon as weather will permit. You said nothing of a school at Marshall. This is a very important item to my mission there; indeed, it was with the view of establishing a permanent and efficient school in that place that I relocated to it as a hopeful field. There are many civilized and native children there that may be gathered into school. And the people are very poor. We must furnish them will all necessary books. I do not know what you do for the other schools in Liberia, but I know what we must expect to do in Marshall. I hope you will be able to allow me such aid in my mission with the assistance of a good teacher. Otherwise my hopes will be all frustrated in that field. I hope in your next to me you will give me definite instruction in regard to my school and how many native boys you will allow me to take under your patronage. Some four

have already applied for attendance. I wait your decision not knowing what the state of your funds will justify. I do not know whether I shall be able to commence building a house for a year hence for I have been obliged to spend the most of the little means I had in hand when I wrote you concerning this matter. I drew a lot from the government to build the church upon and had it deeded to the Board. The lot is worth as much money now in Marshall as you gave to assist in the church building. I think for as much as the property is yours, and the deed I am ready to hand over to your Treasurer at any time you might afford to give more toward the church building. I cannot at least with my poor members, one half congos, pretend to build a permanent church with $50.

Mr. Wright is a man of means and ruling elder in the church, but I do not think he is willing to build the church himself. And should he do it, it will not be the best thing for us. I hope your committee will think of this matter again. We have a temporary house which Rev. Wright and I purchased with our own money at the cost of $25. This will last for some months yet. The classes of books needed are Readers, Spellers, Arithmetic, Grammar, Geography, etc. etc. You may not be in the habit of furnishing these but I assure you if there is any charity in the missions work in Liberia it will--deserved charity to this poor settlement. I hope you will not think I am insisting upon anything that [is] useless or not really necessary.

My health is still feeble. I have fever every week but I am anxious to put my mission in [a] good way before I am obliged to leave the field for my health. I am troubled much with hemorrhoids. This is much against me, having to travel in canoe which excites it every time. I hope there is a prospect of a speedy settlement of the war difficulties in the states. [116]

The following year Thomas is formally stationed in Marshall and teaching a ministerial student in the school for which the Board has yet to furnish requested textbooks or provide funding to support. The Board's insufficient support for educational efforts there discourages Thomas. He and Susanna are frequently ill. His growing anxiety is evident in his February 27 letter.

> Sir, I enclose with this to you a letter given me by my request written by a young man who is studying divinity under my direction. He was taken under the care of our Presbytery last December and recommended by the same Board of education for support. I find him diligent in study and he thus far exhibits a consistent Christian character. He having made considerable proficiency in the study of theology prior to his connection with our Presbytery and having passed a creditable examination in the arts and sciences, classics, etc. We think that we may safely ordain him at the next meeting of our Presbytery. He is anxious to become connected with your Board, and I believe he is willing to occupy any field of usefulness that your executive committee might deem proper to appoint him should you be pleased to employ him. I merely suggest that if your committee has not already appointed a principal for Alexander High School, I would cheerfully recommend Mr. Dillon as being quite competent to occupy that position, he having had extensive experience in teaching. This, however, and the accompanying letter will be for your consideration and examination. I read the letter in part that you may have referenced his own hand writing to gentlemen whose talents we respect.
>
> Our work in this place is prospering. We have a school in operation numbering 21 scholars, all children of settlers except three. They are natives. I deferred taking anymore natives in the school until we would receive further instruction from you. For this reason we may not expect to have an influence for good over them except we have them under our entire control. I consider however that except I can give at least one half of my time to the natives my future prospect in this place is not very hopeful. And this I cannot do unless I have enough boys around me to work my boat when I wish to go to the several towns on the rivers. I cannot hire Americans to do anything like this.

They are either too proud or too lazy or will ask more for one trip than they can generally earn a month.

We are anxious to hear from you your answer to the letter we sent you per *M.C. Stevens* last fall. I allow the young men that are studying divinity under my instruction to teach my school turnabout I pay them; believing that you will appreciate our school in Marshall as to others in Liberia for teaching.

Our church is prospering. From 20 to 30 recaptives attend our church every Sabbath. A number of these are being taught in our Sabbath school. I hope we shall soon be favored with the books which I ordered in my last for school--My wife is in very feeble health. My health is middling. My daughters are quite well. [117]

His April letter and addendum convey his desperation for funds and discouragement about his health.

I send you this hoping it may find you in better health than when you wrote the 18th of December 63. I can say very little at this time that would be interesting to you. My health is not good. Neither that of my wife. We try however to keep on our feet. I think we need not expect to get good health in this country. Concerning my church, we have not increased any the last quarter in embers and I fear very little in spirituality. Our Sabbath school is well attended. Our every day school is prospering. I hope your committee will be able to make an appropriation for my school. I am not able to bear the expense myself. The young men whom the Presbytery put under my instruction are making encouraging progress. The labor that I have to perform this year is too great considering my feeble health. And yet there appears to be no help for it. I need say nothing of our need of devoted missionaries in this country. Your last letter to me states so many reasons why you are not disposed to comply with my request respecting the Marshall mission building that I shall make no further requests in regard to it but wait the movings of

> God's Providence which I know will be wisely ordered. The provisions which you sent me came safely to hand, for which you have our thanks. [118]

His addendum explains mounting health bills.

> One thing more I will mention. My doctor bill has amounted to the handsome sum of $75 and other expenses which have attended my illness will compel me to draw $100 in advance. This thing is as painful to me as it is disagreeable to you but it is caused by a Providence beyond my control. I hope therefore you will not be displeased with me for this unauthorized step for could I help myself I would not do it. [119]

By July Thomas and Susanna are suffering and barely able to work. He requests permission to return to the United States "for the benefit of health" saying "We feel sure that you will sympathize with us--My wife is suffering most." [120] One year furloughs were allowed, usually after a period of eight to ten years. However, the Board made exceptions for critical health conditions. Thomas's furlough is granted, but not soon enough for Susanna who dies before they are able to leave Liberia. According to local history, she is buried in Marshall.

The Board provided housing allowances for missionaries on approved furloughs. Widowed and living in Philadelphia and Reading with his children between 1864 and 1865, Thomas was eligible to receive $450 for the year. [121] In 1864 Thomas and his daughters, Emma and Georgianna, are living in a Philadelphia boarding house at 814 Lombard Street where the rent exceeds what he can afford. "Up to this time we are paying very high board here for $15 per week" he says. "My intention is to get rooms if possible and board ourselves, which I think will make our boarding at a lower rate." [122] Writing to the new corresponding secretary John C. Lowrie (son of Walter Lowrie) in October, Thomas announces he will reside in Reading, PA, for the winter and serve occasionally as preacher at First Colored Presbyterian, his brother's former church which has offered to pay him $15.00 per month. Offended by the paltry offer, he declines to pastor fulltime.

> The church has offered me $15 per month to take charge of their pulpit with the plan that the Board of Foreign Missions are paying me and they therefore have no right giving me half a salary. I told them I would not engage my services to them this winter for such an amount. But as I shall be here this winter I would preach for them and they can make me a present of what they please. I think the pulpit of such uncharitable churches ought to be vacant and for my part I would rather preach for the heathen. [123]

During this time Thomas marries Sarah Miller, a widow with two children, also residing in Reading. Sarah had been married to Civil War soldier, Hutchinson Miller, who served in the 29th Connecticut Colored Infantry. [124] The newlyweds consider returning to Liberia. B.V.R. James encourages Thomas to take charge of the First Presbyterian of Monrovia, the colony's historic church whose membership has dwindled. [125] On March 24, 1866, the now blended Amos family which includes Sarah's 10-year-old son Jacob Franklin and 3 year-old daughter Mary Elizabeth sails from New York City to Monrovia on the *Edith Rose*. The Pennsylvania Colonization Society pays their travel expenses. [126]

On Sunday May 6, 1866, Thomas is installed as pastor of the colony's first Presbyterian Church located at the center of the city where it remains to this day. Edward W. Blyden, then a Professor at Liberia College and celebrated orator, preaches the installation sermon, excerpts of which are published in the *African*

Repository:

A pastor should never forget his duties and privileges as a citizen. He should labor, especially in Liberia, for the upbuilding of his country. The apostle Paul had a tender compassion for all his fellow men, but he felt particularly for his own countrymen. He was very much concerned for the welfare of Israel. He was *patriotic;* and this every pastor should be. While he should carefully avoid all political partisanship, he should so thoroughly inform himself of the history and condition of his country, as always to be able to give his opinions and counsels intelligently, and on the side of progress.

In all countries there is always going on a struggle between the state of things as it is, and the state of things as it is to be, or should be. The struggle is now going on in Liberia; and in this conflict the pastor should be able to guide this people aright. He should constantly inculcate the duty of choosing wise and righteous rulers; and should pray that such rulers may be chosen. He should always be in sympathy with the better social and political movements of the times, though not subservient to them. While he should stand forth as a Reformer, he should not allow that to absorb his character as an Evangelizer. While he should always take an independent stand, he should never allow himself to serve by his sermons any party or administration, not suffer himself to become an advocate or a tool for any political sect. He should carefully avoid all cliqueship, even in the best cause, as trending to fossilize opinions, to foster prejudice more than encourage truth.

And we cannot refrain from insisting most earnestly upon the careful instruction of the young from the pulpit and otherwise. If any country needs the correct training of its youth, Liberia is that country. Everything in the future depends upon them. They are coming up to take possession of the land. Yes, brethren, there is a powerful class coming up in Liberia – a class which, we trust, will be on the side of progress and truth. This class is not confined to any party or sect. It is beyond the influence of clique. It is in no particular portion of the Republic. It is everywhere throughout the land. Its step is light, but as a conquering army it moves on. Soon it will occupy all the places of responsibility and influence in the land. It will hold all the stores – all the offices – all the schools – all the churches; it will cultivate all the farms, carry on all the trade, and sail all the ships. It will stand in every foothold, from the hamlet on the river to the President's mansion, and it will work great changes in the condition of this Republic. This class is composed of the children and youth of the land. They are the architects of Liberia's future. They are coming- we hear their tramp in the distance – they are coming, a noble company of laborers in the cause of Africa's regeneration; they are coming with fresh and vigorous powers, soon to enter upon their arduous toil; and if they are properly trained – if they are allowed to enjoy the light – they will demand with emphasis and effect that the mysterious and useless idols of the past shall be thrown down, and they will construct, on a nobler and truer basis, the religious, social and political character of this nation. And if they should not be properly trained they will also pull down, but it will be with violent and misguided hands – at large from the control of Christian and enlightened principle – and they will reduce to irrecoverable ruins the rising institutions of this last refuge of the persecuted negro. [127]

Thomas's report of his installation is more simplistic and understated. He tells the Board: "I am pleased to be able to say that I am now settled as Pastor of the Church at this place. I was installed the 6th of the present month. The congregation was large and the service interesting. Rev. E.W. Blyden preached the sermon from Acts 20:28." [128]

Throughout his celebrated career as a politician and scholar, Blyden openly condemned the Americo-Liberian practice of excluding the majority native population from the governance of the country. More than a century of discriminating against and exploiting the native population resulted in conflicts and wars that still haunt Liberia. Blyden's selected scripture, Acts 20:28 "Take heed therefore unto yourselves, and to all the flock, over which the Holy Ghost hath made you overseers, to feed the church of God, which he hath purchased with his own blood," seems to foreshadow the consequences of Liberia's divisive social practices. For Thomas, the text may remind him of more immediate challenges of pastoring the church that caters mostly to Americo-Liberians. Membership has dwindled, and the neglected building needs extensive repairs. He observes:

> The membership of this church is quite small. From the best information I can gather it never exceeded 37 and now I do not think it exceeds 20. Yet I am hopeful as I think we can gather a good number into the sabbath school. It has been reopened since I came and the participation is good. [129]

Upon closer inspection, Thomas finds the building in worse condition than he imagined. The window sashes, floors, roof and doors are in advanced stages of decay, a worrisome situation given termite problem in Liberia. The pulpit and seats need to be replaced, and the inside walls need plastering. The estimated repair and replacement costs are high. "The church has authorized me to ask for assistance from abroad," he tells the cash-strapped Board. "Experience teaches me that you have no small concern for our church here, and believing that you will do for us all that you can consistently, therefore appeal to your sympathy and ask your friendly cooperation..." [130]

Thomas's three 1867 letters reflect a discouraged yet devoted pastor who assumes the burden of reviving a dormant congregation, repairing a decaying church building, and trying to build a suitable house in which he and his family can live, all without adequate funds or resources. In January he reports:

> There are 41 or more names of members in our church book. But the largest attendance does not exceed 25 and all of these are not contributors. The numbers of our church are scattered. Some is no attendance, some is another. Our congregation is generally pretty good. We have secured 5 members the year past on the profession of their faith in Christ. I have baptized 4 children. 1 member has been removed by certificate. We have preaching twice on the Sabbath day, prayer meeting Tuesday at the 4 o'clock p.m. lecture, Thursday evening at 7 o'clock. The S. [Sabbath] School of our church is now in a hopeful state. The young people of the church have [enthusiastically] taken hold of the work and are going ahead vigorously--Our church is in the worst condition of any church building in the Cape. [131]

He appeals to Lowrie for funds to renovate the decayed church and to build his house. He pleads for more money, including a personal loan in order to complete his house. Increasingly desperate, he says:

> I am sorry to trouble you further in this matter but I do not know what else to do--You see that I cannot ask for less if I expect to finish the house so I can live in it. And then I shall be much cramped. I hope sir you will consider my plea favorably and give me an answer at the earliest return to it by the first of March. [132]

Thomas next reaches out to Reverend John Brooke Pinney, an official of the New York Colonization Society with whom he met during his 1865 furlough. A long serving Corresponding Secretary to the New York Colonization Society and earlier, the

Pennsylvania Colonization Society, Pinney worked as a missionary in Liberia and in 1833 organized Monrovia's First Presbyterian Church. Knowing Pinney is empathetic to the condition of churches in Liberia, especially his former church, he tells him:

> My dear sir I called at your office in New York and informed you of my intention to endeavor to collect money to repair our Church in Monrovia, which you are aware is in very bad condition. You know I was hindered from my progress by the advice of Doctor Lowrie who thought well at that time to recommend a different course. Two years and over has elapsed and our church is not yet repaired. $200 has been collected for that repair by two generous individuals in the United States and about $150 has been raised here. This is not more than one third what is required [to] complete the repairs. I do not know how this work is to be completed---The Episcopalians are making an effort against in the sense that they have a good church edifice and therefore have no need to make demands for this purpose. This you know has its weight upon poor Liberians who have--been furnished with the gospel and church building gratis. Help us if you can. All things here are as prosperous as could be expected considering the money pressure. We have had but one addition to our church this year. I am trying to build myself a house and in the attempt I am very much cramped for want of means. [133]

A cofounder of Liberia College, Pinney makes a fact-finding trip to Liberia between 1868 and 1869 to report on the condition of churches and schools still supported by the New York and Pennsylvania colonization societies. During this time he visits Thomas often. Soon after his September 1868 arrival, Pinney notices Thomas's declining health and debt burden. He writes in his diary on Friday, September 11:

> ..called on Rev. Mr. Amos, the pastor of Pres. Church and was introduced to Mrs. A. & his three fine children. Rev.

> A. did not look in very fine health. He had moved into his new house, which as often the case in building cost just double. He calculated $1500. He urgently asked me to preach on Sabbath. [134]

The Amoses' new house was located in the Crown Hill section of Monrovia. According to a July 4, 1867 tax receipt, the house on Lot Number 225 was valued at $250.00. [135] Pinney and Thomas discuss church repairs, some for which Pinney helped to raise funds after receiving Thomas's 1867 letter. "Bro. Amos informed me that they had repaired the Pres. Ch. raising $400 in Monrovia & $700 from the Board of Missions; this last voted on the strength of a letter sent to me," Pinney noted on Saturday, September 12. [136]

Concerned about Thomas's health, Pinney checks on him between trips to different areas of the country. "The delay in getting off I used in visiting Mr. Amos, who I found still with some fever but better, "he writes on Monday, November 2." [137] He spent part of his Sunday, November 15 with Thomas.

> After dinner called on Bro. Amos whom I found quite ill & had an interesting talk. He preached for his people at 3 p.m. Bro. A. Herring following with some remarks & closing the services. [138]

That Friday, November 20, close to his time to return to the United States, Pinney "learned that Bro. Amos is quite sick with fever." Following the Civil War Pinney will go on a lecture tour to raise money for his ailing colleague's alma mater, Lincoln University. [139]

***

Thomas's alma mater, now The Lincoln University, awards

him an honorary degree in 1868. While he conveys enthusiasm for the work Ashmun prepared him to do, signs of disappointment surface in his letter to John Miller Dickey that year.

> No doubt you will be glad to hear what we are doing out here, as you have always had a manifest interest in our work in Liberia. As for the church in Monrovia I cannot boast of any great work having been done since I have been here except the building has been repaired at a cost of over $1000. Now and then a member is added to our Communion from some other church. But I have not seen one solitary soul hopefully converted to God through my instrumentality. Since I have been here, there appears to be more regularity and fixedness of purpose among the members yet there is a great want of spirituality. We have a weekly prayer meeting, this our elders very seldom attend. This I find a great drawback as we have very few male members. Rev. A. Herring and the Rev. E.W. Blyden have never attended the prayer meeting since its first organization. These men being the leaders in the church for many years have yet an influence over some house. I find myself in rather a difficult charge. These brethren preach for the Methodists and Baptists about every other Sabbath, of course taking their families and whoever else they can exert an influence over from our church. This does not favor the interests of our church. They seem to envy the prosperity of the church under my ministration. However in despite of their influence we are rather advancing than going back. I pray and trust that we shall ere long see a gracious revival in our Zion. Our churches throughout Liberia has [have] offered inconsequence of the secular spirit of our ministers. We hope to see better days and better things.
>
> Liberia is advancing in intelligence, wealth and national importance, and we think it might now afford a happy home for many of your Black folks who are striving for civil and political rights against a torrent of opposition. My opinion is that the American Blacks will never be fully enfranchised in the United States of America. They are

> weak when compared with the whites, numerically, intellectually and pecuniarily. They therefore must submit to their condition, right or wrong. Why not advise them to seek a home where they can be happy, and enjoy all the rights of free men and be a means to a glorious end in this heathen land and not think themselves an end; but a means in the civilization & Christianization of the multitudes of our benighted brethren.
>
> I am happy to hear that the L [Lincoln] University is prospering. You must feel quite relieved and encouraged to see such blessed results of your efforts. May God bless abundantly the institution, its professors and students, its president and trustees and all its patrons. [140]

By early 1869 Sunday worship attendance has dwindled to 10 or 12, prompting Thomas to lament that a "mission among the heathen" would be preferable. He is ill and suffers from rheumatism which prevents him for regularly conducting church services. Writing to Lowrie, he reports:

> I having recovered in part from a very severe attack of sickness from which I suffered much for three months past, will try to give you an abridged account of our church--- The past year we had preaching regularly every Sabbath morning and afternoon. The attendance was generally pretty good, especially in the morning. Two of our members died the past year, two were received to our Communion, 4 infants were baptized. Our church suffers very much from the unsettled condition of its members. The most active and zealous ones are compelled to go to different parts of the Republic to get employment, so that out of 40 or 46 members we never see present more than half the number. Our Sabbath school is in prosperous condition, the number ranges from thirty to forty. Our weekly prayer meeting is by no means in a prosperous state. My people cannot or will not find time to attend it. Indeed I am discouraged at times to see such want of spirituality and zeal for God. Had I my choice, I would prefer a mission among

> the heathen. This may seem strange to you, but if you knew all my reason it would not so appear.
>
> Since I have been sick my congregation, I am told, has dwindled down to 10 or 12 persons. I feel deep concern for my church, but cannot tell when I shall be able to preach. I am going to take a trip down the coast, shall be gone about 4 weeks. I trust I shall be benefitted in health. I am suffering now from nothing but rheumatism. This however disables me for pastoral duty. I am in very impaired circumstances and am not able to live comfortable, and now, since Elder James is dead and Elder Hilton has moved to Marshall, I need not expect to get much aid from the Church for [they] alone interested themselves about my salary. You are aware that to live in this place is as expensive as to live in New York. I will not further complain least I wear you. I send enclosed with this a small order which I hope you will fill and send at the earliest convenience. [141]

116 The Board considers appointing Thomas as principal of the Alexander High School but questions his fitness for the job, questions he readily addresses by detailing the breadth of his academic studies, not his health. Returning from a health leave during which he visits his former station at Niffau, Thomas says he wants to leave the Monrovia church.

> I have just returned home from the Leeward with health somewhat improved by the voyage. We stopped at Niffau. I went on shore and was kindly received and treated by them. They are very anxious to have a missionary come and live among them. They promise greater things should one come to them. But you are able to judge how much credit may be given to their promises. I should be glad, however, if it is within your power to send a missionary to that station for I am of the opinion that some good by Divine favor might [be] done there. Tom Nimily is yet alive and is the principal man or chief advisor for the whole country of Tarraway, so called by the natives. They now have peace among themselves, throughout their country

and with the natives adjacent. Should this peace continue it would much favor missionary effort. As you know I leave this matter for your consideration.

I shall now refer to yours addressed to the missionaries jointly by the last mail via England. This I read with deep interest what you say concerning the importance of the Alexander High School to our church and country is worthy of our best attention. And what you have said concerning the qualifications necessary to be possessed by the man who shall be the principal of that institution--it may be difficult, however, to find a man in whom all these necessary prerequisites are developed in a very high degree. As to what relates to me in your letter requesting an expression from myself, I confess I am at a loss to know how to answer. You ask whether I think I am competent to fill that position and whether I would be willing to go if appointed. As to the first question I beg to say I shall be glad to refer you to the judgment of my brethren who have had a chance of examining the young men whom I taught, the deputies I mean, John, you are aware was licensed to preach more than a year ago, and--is laboring faithfully in our mission field.

I will state to you what has been my course of study. Geography, History, sacred and profane! Arithmetic, mental and written. Philosophy, physical and moral, also metaphysics. Davy's [Davies] Algebra. Geometry. Logic, Rhetoric, Grammar English, Latin, Greek and Hebrew. Although I have given the dead languages a considerable study yet I do not regard myself as a very proficient teacher of them. The other branches above named I have taught with good success. Those whom I taught in the Languages stood a good examination before Presbytery yet I did not consider them thorough. I have made no mention of these studies which relate exclusively to my Theological course. Should my brethren here and the committee regard me as a suitable one to fill that important place I have no doubt I shall be able to meet your reasonable expectation. Yet I shall be glad if you are able to get a thorough scholar for that place.

> As to my willingness to leave the church at Monrovia I would not hesitate for a moment. But I would not be willing to take the AHS for a salary less than $600. I think I have said quite as much and perhaps more than is necessary for your purpose. I am yours in the bond of Christian fellowship. [142]

Thomas does not get the coveted principal position. Instead, he is hired as a fiscal agent for the Board, a job he holds while pastoring the church he was willing to leave without hesitation. He is candid about his disappointment.

> As your committee has placed in my hands the Financial Agency I can only say that I will endeavor to render satisfaction. I think perhaps it will suit me better than the principalship of the Alexander High School. I have already mailed a letter to you showing my willingness to go to the High School. But as you have said that this appointment supersedes what you said in your previous letter concerning myself and the school you will not regard what I wrote in mine of the 7th--in any other light than complying with your request. [143]

Thomas takes the Board fiscal agent job to supplement the meager salary he receives as pastor, and to repay loans he requested to cover the expense of building his house. His health somewhat improved, he resumes preaching once on the Sabbath and gets around with the help of two canes. He is disgusted with church members' behavior.

> I cannot say that our church is prospering. I greatly fear that the caste question has crept secretly into our church through the influence, especially of Mr. Blyden. For this and other reasons I do not think that my labors are profitable in this church, and I do not think they can be profitable while there is such a diabolical influence being exerted against me, growing out of nothing but prejudice against my influence. The material is not in Monrovia to

> build up a Presbyterian Church out of. The people here are like the colored people in NY and elsewhere they run with the multitude. I must say sir, I am discouraged and sometimes disgusted at the conduct of some of our members, full of religion and no sign of piety. [144]

The "prejudice against my influence" likely refers, in part, to Thomas's position as Deputy Grand Master of the Grand Masonic Lodge of Liberia which he co-founded in 1867 with prominent civic, business and political leaders whom Blyden considered elitists. [145]

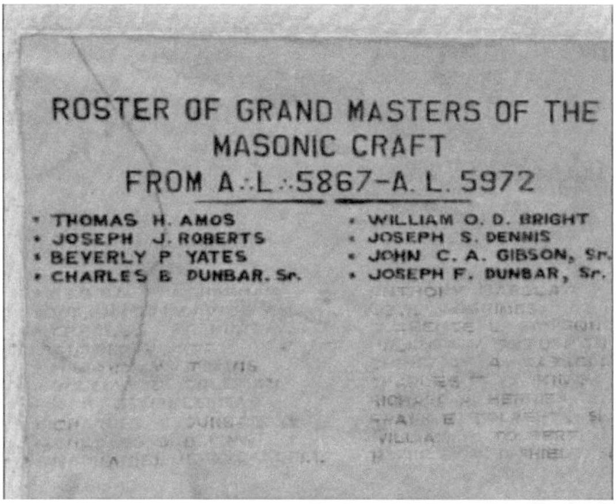

Masonic Temple Memorial Plaque, Monrovia, Liberia.

By mid-May Thomas is "so crippled with rheumatism" that he is confined to his room and seldom able to carry out pastoral duties. "I sometimes think I shall never get good health in Africa" he says. "The doctor forbids that I should preach though I do it sometimes, but not without much inconvenience." [146] Still attending to Board fiscal matters he protests the low appropriations for students, and recommends that quality teachers be hired at the Alexander High School that will educate generations of Liberian leaders.

> The Colonization Society has appropriated $50 to each student per year. Now is not enough unless they could go into the Alexander High School and this they cannot do until we have a teacher there competent to teach them---I am opposed to giving our schools to inferior teachers who cannot lay the foundation of a common English education. I trust the time is not far distant when we shall see better things. [147]

Thomas died sometime between Friday evening July 9 and Saturday morning July 10, 1869. He was 43 years, 7 months and 25 days. "It becomes my melancholy duty to inform you of the death of Rev. Thomas Henry Amos after a lingering illness," Blyden cryptically announces the death of the fellow minister at whose installation he preached just three years ago. "He departed this life on Friday night the 9th--leaving a vacancy in the pulpit of the church of Monrovia and in the office of Treasurer of the Board." [148] Blyden promptly recommends Daniel Warner, a former president of Liberia and a local church elder, to replace Thomas as pastor.

Fellow Presbyterian minister Hopkins W. Erksine is more introspective of his friend's passing, extolling the influence of Thomas's faith, life and his reputation among peers. He says:

> I am again the messenger of sorrow and affliction. Saturday the 10th at half past one o'clock pm a note was handed to me conveying the sad intelligence of the death of our beloved brother Thomas H. Amos in Monrovia. Though I knew he was sick, yet I did [not] expect his death at so early a date. The Wednesday preceding I spent several hours with him and neither of us supposed he was so near the end of his pilgrimage. He was full of hope of immortality. He said he was not afraid to die. The love of God has cast out fear. I feel deeply bereaved however, for within about thirteen months we have been called to mourn the loss

of four valuable members of our little mission family in Liberia-Melville, Boeklen, James [B.V.R.] and Amos. The death of the two last I can hardly realize. And although we believe our loss is their infinite gain, yet their deaths leave a vacuum in our small band that is at present irreparable. [149]

Hopkins W. Erskine, Presbyterian missionary in Liberia. Formerly enslaved in eastern Tennessee, Erskine actively encouraged Blacks to emigrate to his adopted homeland. He was a teacher, farmer and close colleague of James and Thomas Amos. (Library of Congress)

As Erskine assumes the fiscal matters formerly assigned to Thomas, he informs the Board that Sarah Amos plans to soon return to the United States to live with her parents, thus leaving the $550 house mortgage. [150] Missionary H.D. Brown's inquiry about the Amoses' house sheds some light on the state of his deceased colleagues' finances. Specifically, he wants to purchase the mortgage on the house which Sarah plans to soon abandon. He writes:

> I have just seen a mortgage deed given by Rev. Thomas Henry Amos and his wife to the Presbyterian Board of Foreign Missions; executed in the life time of Bro. James. This mortgage for the house and lot his family now occupies in Monrovia having been given for the amount of five hundred and fifty dollars payable in five years and six

months from January 1, 1869. As only the six months are up I write to inquire what action the Board intends taking in the matter. Will the Mission hold this deed until the time is expired and foreclose their mortgage, or will they sell their mortgage right to someone in the country?

Since writing the above I have consulted one of our most distinguished lawyers on the subject, and he says that the Board can retain the deed until the time is expired, transfer it to another for the unexpired time, or present their claim at once to the Administrators for settlement. I am anxious to obtain the premises, and if the Board would transfer the deed to me for the above amount payable in Liberian currency, I would settle their claim at once and thus close the affairs. I would be glad to hear from the Board through you at your earliest convenience concerning the matter that is on--to what course they intend to pursue. I would here remark that the widow with the remainder of the family intends returning to the United States in a few months. [151]

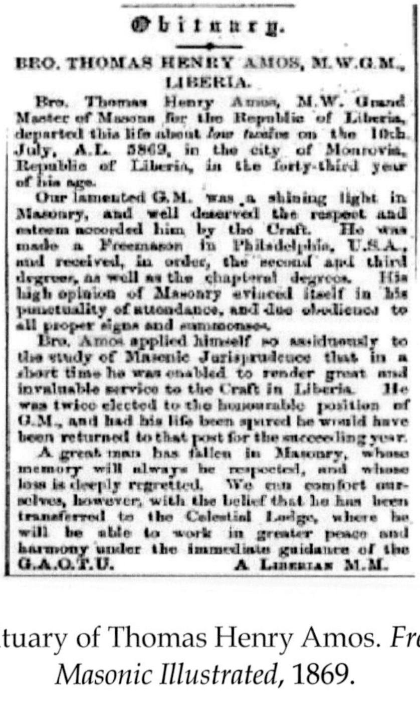

Obituary.

BRO. THOMAS HENRY AMOS, M.W.G.M., LIBERIA.

Bro. Thomas Henry Amos, M.W. Grand Master of Masons for the Republic of Liberia, departed this life about *low twelve* on the 10th July, A.L. 5869, in the city of Monrovia, Republic of Liberia, in the forty-third year of his age.

Our lamented G.M. was a shining light in Masonry, and well deserved the respect and esteem accorded him by the Craft. He was made a Freemason in Philadelphia, U.S.A., and received, in order, the second and third degrees, as well as the chapteral degrees. His high opinion of Masonry evinced itself in his punctuality of attendance, and due obedience to all proper signs and summonses.

Bro. Amos applied himself so assiduously to the study of Masonic Jurisprudence that in a short time he was enabled to render great and invaluable service to the Craft in Liberia. He was twice elected to the honourable position of G.M., and had his life been spared he would have been returned to that post for the succeeding year.

A great man has fallen in Masonry, whose memory will always be respected, and whose loss is deeply regretted. We can comfort ourselves, however, with the belief that he has been transferred to the Celestial Lodge, where he will be able to work in greater peace and harmony under the immediate guidance of the G.A.O.T.U.

A LIBERIAN M.M.

Masonic obituary of Thomas Henry Amos. *Freemason and Masonic Illustrated,* 1869.

Emma, Thomas's daughter from his first marriage, now 21 and an experienced teacher, marries Henry Cooper, a descendant of an early settler family. Emma remains in Liberia. Georgianna returns with her step mother Sarah and step siblings, including Thomas Hunter, to the United States.

Chapter 7

The Night is Far Spent, the Day is at Hand

Romans 13:12

The abolition of slavery in the United States renders the African colonization scheme virtually obsolete, requiring the Ashmun Institute to shift its educational focus. As professions other than the ministry become open to freed Black men, Ashmun's curriculum broadens from training men for service in Africa to training them for vocations, including teaching, law and medicine. [152] Its name change in 1866 to The Lincoln University to honor the emancipator president emphasizes the institution's radically new mission: the education of newly freed African American men. During the annual commencement that year, Major General Oliver Otis Howard, director of the Freedman's Bureau who would become a member of Lincoln's Board of Trustees, urges students to move "onward and upward" in "elevating their race, both in this country and in Africa, but particularly in this country." [153]

While the number of Ashmun graduates emigrating to Liberia to serve as missionaries quickly dwindles, Liberian students, mostly of the Americo-Liberian class, begin to attend Lincoln, followed by the enrollment of members of Liberia's native population in the 1870s. Brick maker and longtime supporter of the institution, Samuel Glasgow, arranges for several native students to study at Lincoln in 1873, some of whom appear in the so dated photograph. [154]

The widowed Sarah Amos settles in Hinsonville and eventually builds a house situated on what is now the edge of

Two Sets of Photographs of Lincoln University Students from Liberia. The first was taken in 1873 when they arrived and the second in 1879. The students are (left to right): Alonzo Miller, Robert Deputie, John Savage and Samuel Sevier. Thomas Henry Amos taught Robert Deputie in Liberia. (Lincoln University)

Lincoln's campus. Called the Amos House, its commemorative plaque recall's Lincoln's humanitarian heritage and relationship with Liberia. It states:

> *In memory of Sarah Hunter Amos widow of Thomas Henry Amos who was a graduate of the first class of Ashmun Institute (later Lincoln University), ordained as a Presbyterian minister and served in Monrovia Liberia as the first Black Presbyterian missionary from 1859-1870. After her husband's death she returned to America and built this house to serve as lodging facilities and dining hall for Lincoln students and worked untiringly for them from 1871-1903. Their son, the late Reverend Thomas Hunter Amos, class of 1887, deeded this house to Lincoln University in 1926 with request it be held as a memorial in honor of this courageous and resourceful woman.*

Born in Monrovia, Liberia, Reverend Thomas Hunter Amos graduated from Lincoln in 1887. He served as President of Harbison College in Abbeville, SC from 1893 to 1906.

Amos House, Lincoln University.
(Photo Credit: Cheryl Renée Gooch)

The young, Monrovia-born Thomas Hunter Amos is raised in this house where African students attending Lincoln are boarded. Thomas enrolls at Lincoln, becomes a Presbyterian minister and eventually serves as president of the church sponsored historically Black Harbison College in Abbeville, South Carolina from 1893 to 1906. Like his father, Reverend Thomas Hunter devotes his life to ministry and education.

Georgianna marries Darius L. Donnell, an 1875 and 1878 Lincoln graduate and Presbyterian minister. The couple sails to Liberia in 1878 where Darius intends to form a mission among the Vey people near the Marfor River. He soon becomes ill and dies from fever on January 21, 1879, confirming "the convictions of the Board that, in enduring the West-Coast climate, the American-born African has no advantages over the Anglo-Saxon" as previously thought. [155] Their son, also named Darius L. Donnell, follows his forefathers' footsteps. He graduates from Lincoln in 1897 and becomes a Presbyterian minister. Georgianna remarried to Amos Washington in 1896 and resided in Baltimore. [156]

Amos Hall, a short distance from the Amos House, was built in 1902 to commemorate brothers James and Thomas, "the first offerings of this Institute laid on the missionary altar," so described by long-serving Lincoln President John B. Rendall. [157]Amos Hall contains the only known image of James, a sculpted frieze atop the entrance. James gazes southward to the grass concealing his prayer stone. Once a quiet sacred grove, the space now complemented by decorative paving stones and comfortable benches is still welcoming. His quizzical expression seems to ask passersby: When singing *we love every inch of her sacred soil, every tree on thy campus green* do you understand the power of unceasing prayer and determination?

Nearby Hosanna Church faces Baltimore Pike, the former Jennersville Road that John Miller Dickey and his wife drove along one Sunday afternoon wondering where to place the

Amos Hall, Lincoln University.

James Ralston Amos. Amos Hall, Lincoln University.
(Photo Credit: Victor Kakulu)

institute to educate talented Black men like James Amos. James and Thomas were Hosanna trustees, experienced abolitionists and well regarded leaders within their community by the time

Dickey took that decisive Sunday afternoon ride into the heart of Hinsonville, a community of praying, self-determined, free people.

Since James and Thomas became Ashmun's first students, Hosanna has welcomed generations of student involvement. Distinguished Civil War veteran and Lincoln alumnus Christian Fleetwood recalled that he and classmates conducted a Sunday afternoon bible study class at Hosanna "which calmly and conclusively settled many devotional points which had puzzled older minds for centuries." [158] More than 150 years after James and Thomas embarked for Liberia to spread the gospel, Lincoln students visit Hosanna; some to worship, some to satisfy their curiosity about the Civil War veterans buried in the atmospheric cemetery; and some to volunteer their services. Some are enamored of the church's storied past as a station on the Underground Railroad. Built in 1843 and rebuilt in 1896, the small church is intact and still opens its doors for worship every Sunday.

Afterword

It's time.

We must not see history as an abstraction. Instead, we must see in its astonishing life force a universe with its deep secrets and hidden treasures, its own sources of anguish, and inevitable measures of triumph.

In September 1953 when I stepped off a Trailways bus onto the campus of Lincoln University, Pennsylvania, I walked through the storied archway into the history books. What I learned as a freshman living in historic Ashmun Hall was an astonishing story of how a long line of my cousins, uncles and grandfathers, driven by galvanizing hope and determination, braved racism, conscience, spirituality and idealism to propel this venerable institution into the annals of history.

As the grandson of Thomas Hunter Amos 'LU 1887, great grandson of Thomas Henry Amos 'LU 1859, and great grandnephew of James Ralston Amos 'LU 1859, I believe *it's time* the story be told of how these resilient men helped establish Ashmun Institute, later Lincoln University, laid the foundation for its distinctive legacy, and the contributions they made to uplift African-ancestored people around the world. *On Africa's Lands*, the forgotten stories of two Lincoln educated men who became missionaries in Liberia, is a long overdue examination of these truths.

The memories of the Amos family, transmitted through the written word and little known period photographs, provide further access to Lincoln's haunting and rich history. The account does more than give the Amoses' perspective on history; it puts a human face on the untold story of slavery's inhumane circumstances, and in doing so allows us to imagine the often unimaginable. Writing with a novelist's artistry, a historian's expertise, and the zeal of an investigative reporter, Dr. Cheryl Gooch puts this history into a timeline to give an immediate link to a world often relegated to the distant past.

Slave masters understood that their social control of the slaves could not be based solely on physical coercion. Knowledge was power, and virtually all slave codes established in the United States set restrictions making it illegal to teach slaves to read or write. The statute passed by the state of North Carolina in 1830—1831, was fairly typical: *"Whereas the teaching of slaves to read and write has a tendency to excite dis-satisfaction in their minds, and to produce insurrection and rebellion, to the manifest injury of the citizens of this State."* While it was against the law to teach a slave to read or write in many slave states, it was good business to teach them carpentry, farming and iron work. Slave and Free states in North America increasingly interested in getting rid of their free Negro populations, encouraged the formation of colonization societies which spawned the return to Africa movement.

In 1821 the America Colonization Society (ACS) dispatched a representative to purchase property from the native population on Cape Mesurado, later known as Liberia. At first, the local leaders were reluctant to surrender their land to strangers, but were forcefully persuaded - some accounts say at gunpoint - to part with a "36 mile long and 3 mile wide" strip of coastal land for trade goods, supplies, weapons and rum worth approximately $300. ACS governed the colony through its representative Jehudi Ashmun, a Methodist missionary. In the common law settlement known as Christopolis, slavery and participation in the slave trade were forbidden. Christopolis was renamed Monrovia after U.S. President James Monroe and the colony was formally called Liberia (the free land).

Meanwhile in U.S. slave states, drums of war were beating louder and would set brother against brother, family against family. On April 12, 1861, the bombardment and surrender of Fort Sumter, near Charleston, South Carolina, started the American Civil War. It is against this backdrop that the Amos brothers flourished, further testimony to their resilience. James and Thomas were free, educated Pennsylvania Negroes. They lived and worked three miles north of that magical Mason Dixon line that divided states where Negroes were born free or as slaves. One would assume they lived in fear of being captured and sold into slavery. My mother often talked about how the Lincoln campus endured 'drive-by' shoot-ups committed by whites. James' thirst for a classical education was not to be quenched when consistent with the norms at the time he was rejected by Princeton Theological Seminary because of his race. Perhaps we should say thank you Princeton as its resistance to Negro admissions would become the impetus for the 1854 founding of Ashmun Institute, the oldest degree granting historically Black university in the United States.

In his writings, Dr. Horace Mann Bond tells a compelling story of how James walked each day the four miles to and from the Presbyterian Church in Oxford for an hour's academic instruction. At the beginning of his walk he would stop in a grove near his house, later the site of Ashmun Hall, where he read the Bible and prayed at a unique stone. James' 'campus altar' was later set in the foundation of the edifice.

The Presbyterians, as did many whites, believed that Negroes were ideally suited to resist disease in Africa and would survive to spread the word of God and convert the so-called heathens. My forefathers who had received a classical education before the Civil War courageously sailed off to Liberia to bring the word of God to the former slaves who had returned to the land of their forebears. Tracing the brothers' surreal journey, we learned that Negroes did in fact get sick and die in Africa as did whites. This important account lays bare how easily history can be whitewashed. The narratives, once dismissed as historical ephemera, reveal that the deck was stacked against the Amos brothers' mission as accounts of Jehudi Ashmun's murderous, authoritarian decisions set the stage for residual anger, hatred and mistrust.

The letters, primary source materials and articles featured in *On Africa's Lands* render a powerful account of mass killings, force-fed religion, confrontations with the Presbyterian Board of Foreign Missions, and the mighty problem of freeing slaves in America and evangelizing the heathen in Africa. Is this not similar to the Crusades of yesteryear and the Jihad of today? The lack of resources and support from home, influenced by the Civil War, severely crippled the Amos brothers' struggle for equality and justice in Liberia. They would die trying.

Growing up in a low rent project in New York's Harlem, I remember spending time with my grandfather, the Reverend Thomas Hunter Amos. He was born in Liberia in 1866 to missionary parents. He grew up on the Lincoln University campus in a house now called The Amos House. My grandfather embodied the bravery of his forbears who faced down racism while working to uplift themselves and their people through education. He was three years old when his father died in Liberia in 1869. From early on, he seemed to know his calling to be a Presbyterian minister and educator. He was a highly educated and brilliant man who read, wrote and spoke English, Greek, Latin and Hebrew. His sermons at the synagogue in Paterson, New Jersey, were delivered in Hebrew from English notes.

Grandpa was a taskmaster. He took pride in quizzing me. I loved and revered him. His friend Dr. W. E. Dubois would visit him at our 3rd floor walkup apartment. After a successful pastorship in Philadelphia, Pennsylvania, Gramps served as the founding president of Harbison College in Abbeville, South Carolina, where he turned a debt ridden school into a debt free, well attended institution for young men of color. In 1906 Dr. Amos and his family, which included my mother Ruth and her twin Fannie, were forced to flee his beloved Harbison in the middle of the night after he learned that KKK mobs were planning to lynch him and burn the school. The school he founded still exists as part of Midlands Technical College in Irmo, South Carolina. My great grandfather Thomas Henry Amos, as his writings reveal, was unwavering in his determination that Liberians, both migrants from America and the indigenous population, receive the highest quality education.

Much has been said about the benevolent white Presbyterians who secured the charter of Lincoln University and for decades dominated its ranks as presidents, professors and trustees. Until now, the legend of their "good works" has dominated The Lincoln University story. In *On Africa's Lands* we hear the authentic voices of James and Thomas Amos; their unvarnished stories in their own words about life as pioneering missionaries in Liberia. More than 130 years have elapsed since ratification of the Thirteenth Amendment to the U.S. Constitution declared slavery illegal in the United States, yet America is still wrestling with the legacy of slavery. Their stories of struggle and triumph in a post slavery era offer an important contribution to American historiography. *On Africa's Lands* will undoubtedly enrich our common memory and widen our horizons as Americans.

Ernest C. Levister, Jr. LU' 1958

Notes

Chapter 1

1 John Miller Dickey, *Ethiopia Shall Soon Stretch Out Her Hand Unto God Outlines of a Delivered in the Presbyterian Church in Oxford, Pennsylvania,* 1853, Langston Hughes Memorial Library Special Collections and Archives, Lincoln University. Dickey's sermon was intended to justify the founding of a school for the Christian training of colored youth. Psalm 68:31 was a favorite colonization text referring to God's plan being fulfilled in Africa. Dickey believed the institution to be a part of the divine plan and that Black men were called to spread the gospel in Africa.

2 Pauli Murray, *Proud Shoes: The Story of an American Family* (Boston, MA: Beacon Press, 1999), 94-95 and William C. Kashatus, *Just Over the Line: Chester County and the Underground Railroad* (West Chester, PA: Chester County Historical Society, 2002), 94-96.

3 Horace Mann Bond, *Education for Freedom: A History of Lincoln University* (Princeton, NJ: Princeton University Press for Lincoln University, 1976), 210.

4 Cheryl Renée Gooch, "On Africa's Lands: The Shared Humanitarian Heritage of Hosanna Church and Lincoln University," *Lincoln Journal of Social and Political Thought* 8.2 (2013): 11-38.

5 William Decker Johnson, *Lincoln University: The Nation's First Pledge of Emancipation* (Philadelphia, PA: William D. Johnson, 1867), 8. In this celebratory history of his alma mater, Johnson reiterates the frequently told story of Samuel Glasgow making the bricks for Ashmun Hall.

6 Pauli Murray, 94-95.

7 Frederick Douglass, *The Frederick Douglass Papers. Series 3: Correspondence, Volume 1: 1842-52,* McKivigan, John R. ed. (New Haven, CT: Yale University Press, 2009), 28.

8 Kashatus, 94-96; Bond, *Education for Freedom*; and Marianne H. Russo and Paul A. Russo, *Hinsonville, A Community at the Crossroads: The Story of a Nineteenth-Century African-American Village* (Selinsgrove, PA: Susquehanna University Press, 2005).

9 John Thomas, Edwin Coates, and Edwin Fussell, "Chester County Conventions: To the Abolitionists of Chester County and Vicinity," *National Anti-Slavery Standard,* 11 February 1844,179.

10 Giles Badger Stebbins, letter to Charles C. Burleigh, January 8, 1854. Reprinted in the *Pennsylvania Freeman*, February 2, 1854.

11 Giles Badger Stebbins, *Facts and Opinions Touching the Real Origin, Character, and Influence of the American Colonization Movement* (New York: Negro Universities Press, 1969), 172.

12 George Bogue Carr, *John Miller Dickey, D.D., His Life and Times.* Finney, William P. ed. (Philadelphia, PA: Westminster Press, 1929), 162.

13 Although not the focus of this book, Miller and the detailed history of his life and missionary work in Liberia are covered by Nancy E. Aiken and Michel S. Perdreau in "Armistead Miller: Presbyterian Missionary and Emigrant to Liberia," originally published in the *Journal of the Afro-American Historical and Genealogical Society*, 15. 2, 1996.

The digital version of this article < http://www.seorf.ohiou.edu/~xx057/miller.htm>, accessed 8 November 2013. See also Reginald H. Pitts's discussion of Millers' Liberian efforts in "Founders and Focus of the Ashmun Collegiate Institute for Colored Youth Chester County, Pennsylvania, 1854-1866." *Journal of the Afro-American Historical and Genealogical Society* 13.3/4 (1994): 144-164.

14 *Pennsylvania Colonization Society Minutes, 1856-1864*, Special Collections Archive, Lincoln University. <http://

www.lincoln.edu/library/specialcollections/society/1856-1864.pdf>, accessed 5 January, 2014; *Manual of the Board of Foreign Missions of the Presbyterian Church in the U.S.A*, New York, NY: 1889 <https://archive.org/details/manualofboardoff00pres>, accessed 5 January 2014.

15 "Emigrants for Liberia," *Baltimore American*, 12 May 1859, 1; and *From Greenland's Icy Mountains*, written by Reginald Heber, 1819. <http://www.hymnary.org/text/from_greenlands_icy_mountains>, accessed 13 October 2013.

16 "Emigrants for Liberia," 1.

Chapter 2

17 Augustus Washington, letter to the editors, *New York Tribune*, July 03, 1851<http://teachingamericanhistory.org/library/document/african-colonization-by-a-man-of-color/>, accessed 14 November, 2013. Washington's surviving daguerreotypes comprised a 1999 National Portrait Gallery exhibit. See Ann M. Shumard, *A Durable Memento: Portraits by Augustus Washington, African American Daguerreotypist* (Washington, DC: National Portrait Gallery, 1999).

18 Johnson, 25-26.

19 *Manual of the Board of Foreign Missions of the Presbyterian Church in the U.S.A*, New York, NY: 1889 <https://archive.org/details/manualofboardoff00pres>, accessed 5 January 2014.

20 *Historical Sketches of the Missions Under the Care of the Board of Foreign Missions of the Presbyterian Church U.S.A*, Philadelphia, PA: 1897 < https://archive.org/details/historicalsketch00pres>, accessed 5 January 2014.

21 Thomas Henry Amos, letter to John Leighton Wilson, September 23, 1859.

22 Ibid.

23 Thomas Henry Amos, addendum to letter to Presbyterian Board of Foreign Missions, December 27, 1859.

24 James Ralston Amos, letter to John Leighton Wilson, December 9, 1859.

25 Ibid.

26 Ibid.

27 Ibid.

28 James Ralston Amos and Thomas Henry Amos, letter to John Leighton Wilson, February 9, 1860.

29 James Ralston Amos and Thomas Henry Amos, letter to John Leighton Wilson, April 5, 1860.

30 Thomas Henry Amos and James Ralston Amos letter to John Leighton Wilson, August 18, 1860.

31 Thomas Henry Amos, letter to John Leighton Wilson, October 11, 1860.

32 James Ralston Amos, letter to John Leighton Wilson, December 5, 1860.

33 Thomas Henry Amos, letter to John Leighton Wilson, January 5, 1861.

34 Thomas Henry Amos, letter to John Leighton Wilson, January 5, 1861.

35 Thomas Henry Amos and James Ralston Amos, letter to John Leighton Wilson, March 1, 1861.

36 Thomas Henry Amos, letter to John Leighton Wilson, April 6, 1861.

37 Wulah, Teah, *The Forgotten Liberian: History of Indigenous Tribes* (Bloomington, IN: Author House, 2005).

38 James Ralston Amos, letter to John Leighton

Wilson, July 19, 1861.

39 James Ralston Amos and Thomas Henry Amos, letter to Walter Lowrie, October 23, 1861.

40 Hampden C. Dubose, *Memoirs of Rev. JohnLeighton Wilson, Missionary to Africa and Secretary of Foreign Missions* (Richmond, VA: Presbyterian Committee of Publication), 1895, 97 <http://openlibrary.org/books/OL14022351M/Memoirs_of_Rev._John_Leighton_Wilson>, accessed 5 October 2012.

41 James Ralston Amos and Thomas Henry Amos, letter to Walter Lowrie, October 23, 1861.

42 B.V.R. James, letter to Walter Lowrie, December 7, 1861.

43 Ibid.

44 Donald F. Roth, "The "Black Man's Burden": The Racial Background of Afro-American Missionaries and Africa," in Jacobs, Sylvia M., ed., *Black Americans and the Missionary Movement in Africa* (Westport, CT: Greenwood Press, 1982), 36; Liam Riordan, "Passing as Black/Passing as Christian: African-America Religious Autonomy in Early Republican Delaware," *Pennsylvania History* 64.5 (1997): 207-229.

45 Liberia Declaration of Independence, July 16, 1847.

46 Lewis V. Baldwin, "Through the Prism of History: The Many Dimensions of Big Quarterly," *August Quarterly*, 1990, 5.

47 Alice Dunbar-Nelson, "Big Quarterly in Wilmington, Del.," *Candid*, October, 1938, 9-13.

48 Abraham D. Shad, Peter Spencer, and William S. Thomas, "Address of the Free People of Color of the Borough of Wilmington, Delaware," *Delaware Free Press*, August 6, 1831, 2.

49 Peter Spencer, *The African Union Hymn-Book*.

Wilmington, DE: Porter and Noff, 1839, 97.

Chapter 3

50 Samuel Glasgow, letter to Jesse E. Glasgow, November 3, 1862. Reprinted in *African Repository Annual Report*. Washington, DC: American Colonization Society, August, 1863, 236.

51 Thomas Henry Amos, letter to Walter Lowrie, February 20, 1862.

52 B.V. R. James, letter to Walter Lowrie, March 10, 1862.

53 B.V. R. James, letter to Walter Lowrie, March 10, 1862.

54 Thomas Henry Amos, letter to Walter Lowrie, March 17, 1862.

55 Thomas Henry Amos, letter to Walter Lowrie, March 17, 1862.

56 James Ralston Amos, letter to Walter Lowrie, April 21, 1862.

57 *Annual Report of the Board of Foreign Missions of the Presbyterian Church,*1862<http://books.google.com/books>, accessed 13 November 2013.

58 Ibid.

59 According to James's nephew, the Reverend Thomas Hunter Amos, his grandmother "trucked her way from a cabin on a farm where the McDowell's Mill was situated to the study of the minister of the Faggs Manor church who conducted a school for the children." See *Thomas Hunter Amos Family Papers*. See also Faggs Manor Presbyterian Church, Cochranville, PA Session Minutes and Records, Volume 2, 1835-1859, Presbyterian

Historical Society, and William B. Noble, H.F.C. Heagey and Musetta E., McClellan, *A History of Faggs Manor United Presbyterian Church, 1730-1980*, Cochranville, PA: The Church, 1980. According to the Fagg's Manor Session Minutes and Records, a Sarah Jane Hunter, "colored," joined the church on September 25, 1847, two years before the academy opened. She may have been the mother of the Amos brothers whose descendants sometimes use "Hunter"as a part of their names. Faggs Manor records show several "colored" members during this period.

60 Charles Hodge, letter to John Miller Dickey, May 5, 1852, Langston Hughes Memorial Library Special Collections and Archives, Lincoln University.

61 Carr, 161.

62 Johnson, 14. He also pastored the First African Presbyterian Church in Reading, PA, while enrolled at Ashmun, a position likely secured through his affiliation with the Presbyterian Church supported Ashmun.; *Washington Presbyterian Church (USA) of Reading, PA History*, 1998. The original name was "First African Presbyterian Church of Reading." Amos served as pastor for approximately two years, from 1857 to 1859, before emigrating to Liberia.

63 James Ralston Amos, letter to Walter Lowrie, September 2, 1862.

64 James Ralston Amos, letter to Walter Lowrie, September 10, 1862.

65 Thomas Henry Amos, letter to Walter Lowrie, September 8, 1862.

66 James Ralston Amos, letter to Walter Lowrie, October 31, 1862.

67 Ibid.

68 Ibid.

69 Ibid.

70 James Ralston Amos, letter to Walter Lowrie, November 4, 1862.

71 Ibid.

72 James Ralston Amos, letter to Walter Lowrie, November 12, 1862.

73 James Ralston Amos, letter to Walter Lowrie, December 26, 1862.

Chapter 4

74 Thomas Henry Amos, letter to Walter Lowrie, January 5, 1863.

75 Thomas Henry Amos, letter to Walter Lowrie, January 30, 1863.

76 Niffau," *African Repository,* September 1862, 265-266.

77 "Niffau," *African Repository,* August 1863, 236.

78 Tom W. Shick, "Rhetoric and Reality: Colonization and Afro-American Missionaries in early Nineteenth-Century Liberia," in Sylvia M. Jacobs, ed., *Black Americans and the Missionary Movement in Africa* (Westport, CT: Greenwood Press, 1982), 47.

79 Jehudi Ashmun, *History of the American Colony in Liberia* (Washington, DC: Way & Gideon, 1826), 28-29.

80 Ibid, 36.

81 Ibid, 38.

82 Giles Badger Stebbins, *Facts and Opinions Touching the Real Origin, Character, and Influence of the American Colonization Movement*, 172.

83 Ashmun, 24.

84 Alexander Priestley Camphor, *Missionary Story Sketches: Folk-lore from Africa* (Cincinnati, OH: Jennings and Graham, 1909), 162.

85 Ibid, 170.

86 James Ralston Amos, letter to John Leighton Wilson, July 19, 1861.

87 Camphor, 109.

88 Ibid, 131.

89 James Ralston Amos, letter to John Leighton Wilson, July 19, 1861.

90 Camphor, 288-290.

91 Ibid, 295-296.

Chapter 5

92 Samuel Glasgow, letter to Jesse E. Glasgow, February 15, 1863. Reprinted in *African Repository Annual Report,* August, 1863, 314-315.

93 Ibid.

94 James Ralston Amos, letter to Walter Lowrie, February 7, 1863.

95 Ibid.

96 Ibid.

97 James Ralston Amos, letter to Walter Lowrie, February n.d., 1863.

98 James Ralston Amos, letter to Walter Lowrie, April

3, 1863.

99 Ibid.

100 Ibid.

101 James Ralston Amos, letter to Walter Lowrie, May 5, 1863.

102 Ibid.

103 James Ralston Amos, letter to Walter Lowrie, July 1, 1863.

104 James Ralston Amos, letter to Walter Lowrie, July 8, 1863.

105 James Ralston Amos, letter to Walter Lowrie, August 26, 1863.

106 James Ralston Amos, letter to Walter Lowrie, November 10, 1863.

107 James Ralston Amos, letter to Walter Lowrie, March 14, 1864.

108 Joseph M. Wilson, *The Presbyterian Historical Almanac and Annual Remembrancer of the Church,* Philadelphia, PA: Joseph M. Wilson, 1866, 90-91 <http://www.archive.org/stream/presbyterianhist08wils/presbyterianhist08wils_djvu.txt>, accessed 10 October 2013.

109 Ibid.

Chapter 6

110 Thomas Henry Amos, letter to Walter Lowrie, April 30, 1863.

111 Ibid.

112 Ibid.

113 Ibid.

114 Thomas Henry Amos, letter to Walter Lowrie, June 2, 1863.

115 Thomas Henry Amos, letter to Walter Lowrie, June 8, 1863.

116 Thomas Henry Amos, letter to Walter Lowrie, September 28, 1863.

117 Thomas Henry Amos, letter to Walter Lowrie, February 27, 1864.

118 Thomas Henry Amos, letter to Walter Lowrie, April 4, 1864.

119 Thomas Henry Amos, letter to Walter Lowrie, nd., 1864.

120 Thomas Henry Amos, letter to Walter Lowrie, July 18, 1864.

121 *Manual of the Board of Foreign Missions of the Presbyterian Church in the U.S.A*, New York, NY: 1889 <https://archive.org/details/manualofboardoff00pres>, accessed 5 January 2014.

122 Thomas Henry Amos, letter to Walter Lowrie, July 24, 1865.

123 Thomas Henry Amos, letter to John C. Lowrie, October 26, 1865.

124 According to Sarah's widow pension claim to the Bureau of Pensions on April 30, 1907, Miller died on February 24, 1865 from combat wounds to the head and arm. She and Thomas Amos married on October 12, 1865.

125 Thomas Henry Amos, letter to John C. Lowrie, November 2, 1865.

126 *Pennsylvania Colonization Society Minutes, 1864-1877*. Langston Hughes Memorial Library Special Collections and Archives, Lincoln University. <http://www.lincoln.edu/library/specialcollections/society/1864-1877.pdf>, accessed 2 February, 2014.

127 "The Pastor's Work, A Sermon by Rev. Blyden," *African Repository*, August 1866, 246-247.

128 Thomas Henry Amos, letter to John C. Lowrie, May 25, 1866.

129 Ibid.

130 Ibid.

131 Thomas Henry Amos, letter to John C. Lowrie, January 30, 1867.

132 Thomas Henry Amos, letter to John C. Lowrie, February n.d., 1867.

133 Thomas Henry Amos, letter to John B. Pinney, October 25, 1867.

134 John Brooke Pinney journal, Schomburg Center for Research in Black Culture, The New York Public Library.

135 *Thomas Hunter Amos Family Papers.*

136 John Brooke Pinney journal.

137 Ibid.

138 Ibid.

139 Ibid. See also, John Dunlap Wells, *In Memoriam: Rev. John Brooke Pinney, LL.D.*, New York Colonization Society, 1882, 9.

140 Thomas Henry Amos, letter to John M. Dickey, July 11, 1868.

141 Thomas Henry Amos, letter to John C. Lowrie, February 1, 1869.

142 Thomas Henry Amos, letter to John C. Lowrie, April 7, 1869.

143 Thomas Henry Amos, letter to John C. Lowrie, April 13 & May 11, 1869.

144 Thomas Henry Amos, letter to John C. Lowrie, May 7, 1869.

145 Grand Lodge of Masons, Republic of Liberia, <http://www.grandlodgeofliberia.org/pages1.php?pgID=36>, accessed 30 December 2013.

146 Thomas Henry Amos, letter to John C. Lowrie, May 18, 1869.

147 Ibid.

148 Edward Wilmot Blyden, letter to John C. Lowrie, July 12, 1869.

149 Hopkins W. Erskine, letter to John C. Lowrie, July 12, 1869; According to *The Record of the Presbyterian Church in the United States of America*, Philadelphia, PA: Presbyterian Board of Publication, 1869, <http://books.google.com/books>, accessed 14 December 2012, Mellville, Boeklen, and James were "coloured men of the best character, and all of them being devoted to the work of missions..." and "In hardly any country are such labourers more needed."

150 Hopkins W. Erskine, letter to John C. Lowrie, August 11, 1869.

151 H.D. Brown, letter to William Rankin, Jr., August 18, 1869.

Chapter 7

152 Andrew E. Murray, "The Founding of Lincoln University," *Journal of Presbyterian History* 51 (1973): 410.

153 "The Celebration of Lincoln University," *American Republican*, July, 3, 1866. 1853-1874 University<http://contentdm.auctr.edu/cdm/compoundobject/collection/lupa/id/2044/rec/1>, accessed 21 September 2013.

154 Reginald H. Pitts, "Founders and Focus of the Ashmun Collegiate Institute for Colored Youth Chester County, Pennsylvania, 1854-1866," *Journal of the Afro-American Historical and Genealogical Society* 13.3/4 (1994): 157; Bond, 490-491.

155 *Minutes of the United Presbyterian Church in the U.S.A.*, 1879, 687. <http://books.google.com/books>, accessed 2 February 2014.

156 *Catalogue of the Officers and Students of Lincoln University, 1877-78* and *Statistical Catalogue of the Students of the Collegiate and Theological Departments of Lincoln University*, 1912, Langston Hughes Memorial Library Special Collections and Archives, Lincoln University; United States Census 1900, Baltimore City, Maryland, lists seamstress as Georgianna's profession. Darius is listed as a minister and Amos as a waiter in the 1905 Baltimore City Directory.

157 David McBride, "Africa's Elevation and Changing Racial Thought at Lincoln University, 1854-1886," *Journal of Negro History* 62.4 (1977): 364.

158 Christian Fleetwood, letter to Isaac N. Rendall, March 21, 1911. Langston Hughes Memorial Library Special Collections and Archives, Lincoln University.

Bibliography

Aiken, Nancy E. and Perdreau, Michel S. "Armistead Miller: Presbyterian Missionary and Emigrant to Liberia." *Journal of the Afro-American Historical and Genealogical Society*, 15. (1996). <http://www.seorf.ohiou.edu/~xx057/miller.htm>, accessed 8 November 2013.

Thomas Henry Amos, letter to John M. Dickey, July 11, 1868. Langston Hughes Memorial Library Special Collections and Archives, Lincoln University.

Thomas Hunter Amos Family Papers.

Annual Report of the Board of Foreign Missions of the Presbyterian Church, 1862, 15. <http://books.google.com/books>, accessed 13 November 2013.

Ashmun, Jehudi. *History of the American Colony in Liberia.* Washington, DC: Way & Gideon, 1826, 28-29; 36-38.

Baldwin, Lewis V. "Through the Prism of History: The Many Dimensions of Big Quarterly," *August Quarterly*, 1990.

Bond, Horace Mann. *Education for Freedom: A History of Lincoln University*. Princeton, NJ: Princeton University Press for Lincoln University, 1976.

Camphor, Alexander Priestley. *Missionary Story Sketches: Folk-lore from Africa*. Cincinnati, OH: Jennings and Graham, 1909.

Carr, George Bogue. *John Miller Dickey, D.D., His Life and Times.* Finney, William P. ed. Philadelphia, PA: Westminster Press, 1929, 162.

Catalogue of the Officers and Students of Lincoln University, 1877-78. Langston Hughes Memorial Library Special Collections and Archives, Lincoln University.

Dickey, John Miller. *Ethiopia Shall Soon Stretch Out Her Hand Unto God: Outlines of a Delivered in the Presbyterian Church in Oxford, Pennsylvania*, 1853. Langston Hughes Memorial Library Special Collections and Archives, Lincoln University.

Douglass, Frederick. *The Frederick Douglass Papers. Series 3: Correspondence, Volume 1:1842-52*. McKivigan, John R. ed. New Haven, CT: Yale University Press, 2009.

Dubose, Hampden C. *Memoirs of Rev. John Leighton Wilson, Missionary to Africa and Secretary of Foreign Missions*. Richmond, VA: Presbyterian Committee of Publication, 1895, 97. <http://openlibrary.org/books/OL14022351M/Memoirs_of_Rev._John_Leighton_Wilson>, accessed 5 October 2012.

"Emigrants for Liberia," *Baltimore American*, 12 May 1859, 1.

Faggs Manor Presbyterian Church, Cochranville, PA Session Minutes and Records, Volume 2, 1835-1859. Presbyterian Historical Society, Philadelphia, PA.

Christian Fleetwood, letter to Isaac N. Rendall, March 21, 1911. Langston Hughes Memorial Library Special Collections and Archives, Lincoln University.

From Greenland's Icy Mountains, written by Reginald Heber, 1819. <http://www.hymnary.org/text/from_greenlands_icy_mountains>, accessed 13 October 2013.

Samuel Glasgow, letter to Jesse E. Glasgow, November 3, 1862. Reprinted in *African Repository Annual Report*. Washington, DC: American Colonization Society, August, 1863, 236.

Samuel Glasgow, letter to Jesse E. Glasgow, February 15, 1863. Reprinted in *African Repository Annual Report,* August, 1863, 314-315.

Gooch, Cheryl Renée. "On Africa's Lands: The Shared Humanitarian Heritage of Hosanna Church and Lincoln University." *Lincoln Journal of Social and Political Thought* 8.2 (2013): 11-38.

Grand Lodge of Masons, Republic of Liberia.<http://www.grandlodgeofliberia.org/pages1.php?pgID=36>, accessed 30 December 2013.

Historical Sketches of the Missions Under the Care of the Board of Foreign Missions of the Presbyterian Church U.S.A, Philadelphia, PA: 1897. < https://archive.org/details/historicalsketch00pres>, accessed 5 January 2014.

Charles Hodge, letter to John Miller Dickey, May 5, 1852. Langston Hughes Memorial Library Special Collections and Archives, Lincoln University.

Johnson, William Decker. *Lincoln University: The Nation's First Pledge of Emancipation*. Philadelphia, PA: William D. Johnson, 1867.

Kashatus, William C. *Just Over the Line: Chester County and the Underground Railroad.* West Chester, PA: Chester County Historical Society, 2002, 94-96.

Liberia Declaration of Independence, July 16, 1847.

McBride, David. "Africa's Elevation and Changing Racial Thought at Lincoln University, 1854-1886." *Journal of Negro History* 62.4 (1977): 363-377.

Manual of the Board of Foreign Missions of the Presbyterian Church in the U.S.A, New York, NY: 1889. <https://archive.org/details/manualofboardoff00pres>, accessed 5 January 2014.

Minutes of the United Presbyterian Church in the U.S.A., 1879, 687. <http://books.google.com/books>, accessed 2 February 2014.

Murray, Andrew E. "The Founding of Lincoln University." *Journal of Presbyterian History* 51 (1973): 392-410.

Murray, Pauli. *Proud Shoes: The Story of an American Family*. Boston, MA: Beacon Press, 1999.

Nelson-Dunbar, Alice. "Big Quarterly in Wilmington, Del.," *Candid*, October, 1938. Reprint of 1932 article.

"Niffau," *African Repository*, September 1862, 265-266.

"Niffau," *African Repository*, August 1863, 236.

Nobel, William B., Heagey, H.F.C. and McClellan, Musetta E. *A History of Faggs Manor United Presbyterian Church, 1730-1980*. Cochranville, PA: The Church, 1980.

Pennsylvania Colonization Society Minutes, 1856-1864. Langston Hughes Memorial Library Special Collections and Archives, Lincoln University. <http://www.lincoln.edu/library/specialcollections/society/1856-1864.pdf>, accessed 5 January, 2014.

Pennsylvania Colonization Society Minutes, 1864-1877. Langston Hughes Memorial Library Special Collections and Archives, Lincoln University. <http://www.lincoln.edu/library/specialcollections/society/1864-1877.pdf>, accessed 2 February, 2014.

Pinney, John Brooke. 1868-1869 journal. Schomburg Center for Research in Black Culture, The New York Public Library.

Pitts, Reginald H. "Founders and Focus of the Ashmun Collegiate Institute for Colored Youth Chester County, Pennsylvania, 1854-1866." *Journal of the Afro American Historical and Genealogical Society* 13.3/4 (1994): 144-164.

Riordan, Liam. "Passing as Black/Passing as Christian: African-America Religious Autonomy in Early Republican Delaware." *Pennsylvania History* 64.5 (1997): 207-229.

Roth, Donald F "The "Black Man's Burden": The Racial Background of Afro American Missionaries and Africa." In Jacobs, Sylvia M., ed. *Black Americans and the Missionary Movement in Africa.* Westport, CT: Greenwood Press, 1982: 131-37.

Russo, Marianne H. and Russo, Paul A. *Hinsonville, A Community at the Crossroads: The Story of a Nineteenth-Century African-American Village*. Selinsgrove, PA: Susquehanna University Press, 2005.

Shad, Abraham D., Spencer, Peter, and Thomas, William S. "Address of the Free People of Color of the Borough of Wilmington, Delaware," *Delaware Free Press*, August 6, 1831, 1-2.

Shumard, Ann M. *A Durable Memento: Portraits by Augustus Washington, African American Daguerreotypist.* Washington, DC: National Portrait Gallery, 1999.

Spencer, Peter. *The African Union Hymn-Book*. Wilmington, DE: Porter and Noff, 1839, 93.

Statistical Catalogue of the Students of the Collegiate and Theological Departments of Lincoln University, 1912. Langston Hughes Memorial Library Special Collections and Archives, Lincoln University.

Giles Badger Stebbins, letter to Letter to Charles C. Burleigh, January 8, 1854. Reprinted in the *Pennsylvania Freeman,* February 2, 1854.

Stebbins, Giles Badger. *Facts and Opinions Touching the Real Origin, Character, and Influence of the American Colonization Movement.* New York: Negro Universities Press, 1969, 172.

"The Celebration of Lincoln University." *American Republican,* July, 3, 1866. Newspaper Clippings of Ashmun Institute & Lincoln 1853-1874, http://contentdm.auctr.edu/cdm/compoundobject/collection/lupa/id/2044?rec/1>, accessed 21 September 2013.

"The Pastor's Work, A Sermon by Rev. Blyden." *African Repository*, August 1866, 246-247.

The Record of the Presbyterian Church in the United States of America. Philadelphia, PA: Presbyterian Board of Publication, 1869, <http://books.google.com/books>, accessed 14 December 2012.

Thomas, John, Coates, Edwin and Fussell, Edwin. "Chester County Conventions: To the Abolitionists of Chester County and Vicinity." *National Anti-Slavery Standard,* 11 February 1844, 179.

Augustus Washington, letter to the editors, *New York Tribune*, July 03, 1851. <http://teachingamericanhistory.org/library/document/african-colonization-by-a-man-of-color/>, accessed 14 November, 2013.

Washington Presbyterian Church (USA) of Reading, PA History, 1998.

Wells, John Dunlap. *In Memoriam: Rev. John Brooke Pinney, LL.D.* New York Colonization Society, 1882, 9.

Wilson, Joseph M. *The Presbyterian Historical Almanac and Annual Remembrancer of the Church.* Philadelphia, PA: Joseph M. Wilson, 1866, 90-91. <http://www.archive.org/stream/presbyterianhist08wils/presbyterianhistwils_djvu.txt>, accessed 10 October 2013.

Wulah, Teah. *The Forgotten Liberian: History of Indigenous Tribes.* Bloomington, IN: Author House, 2005.

List of Amos Brothers and Related Letters

Board of Foreign Missions Correspondence and Reports 1833-1911, Presbyterian Historical Society, Philadelphia, PA.

In order cited:

Thomas Henry Amos, letter to John Leighton Wilson, September 23, 1859.

James Ralston Amos, letter to John Leighton Wilson, December 9, 1859.

Thomas Henry Amos, letter to John Leighton Wilson, December 27, 1859.

Thomas Henry Amos, addendum to letter to John Leighton Wilson, December 27, 1859.

James Ralston Amos and Thomas Henry Amos, letter to John Leighton Wilson, February 9, 1860.

James Ralston Amos and Thomas Henry Amos, letter to John Leighton Wilson, April 5, 1860.

Thomas Henry Amos and James Ralston Amos, letter to John Leighton Wilson, August 18, 1860.

Thomas Henry Amos, letter to John Leighton Wilson, October 11, 1860.

James Ralston Amos, letter to John Leighton Wilson, December 5, 1860.

Thomas Henry Amos, letter to John Leighton Wilson, January 5, 1861.

James Ralston Amos, letter to John Leighton Wilson, February 1,

1861.

Thomas Henry Amos and James Ralston Amos, letter to John Leighton Wilson, March 1, 1861.

Thomas Henry Amos, letter to John Leighton Wilson, April 6, 1861.

James Ralston Amos, letter to John Leighton Wilson, July 19, 1861.

James Ralston Amos and Thomas Henry Amos, letter to Walter Lowrie, October 23, 1861.

B.V. R. James, letter to Walter Lowrie, December 7, 1861.

Thomas Henry Amos, letter to Walter Lowrie, February 20, 1862.

B.V. R. James, letter to Walter Lowrie, March 10, 1862.

Thomas Henry Amos, letter to Walter Lowrie, March 17, 1862.

James Ralston Amos, letter to Walter Lowrie, April 21, 1862.

B.V. R. James, letter to Walter Lowrie, April 22, 1862.

James Ralston Amos, letter to Walter Lowrie, September 2, 1862.

Thomas Henry Amos, letter to Walter Lowrie, September 8, 1862.

James Ralston Amos, letter to Walter Lowrie, September 10, 1862.

James Ralston Amos, letter to Walter Lowrie, October 31, 1862.

James Ralston Amos, letter to Walter Lowrie, November 4, 1862.

James Ralston Amos, letter to Walter Lowrie, November 12, 1862.

James Ralston Amos, letter to Walter Lowrie, December 26, 1862.

Thomas Henry Amos, letter to Walter Lowrie, January 5, 1863.

Thomas Henry Amos, letter to Walter Lowrie, January 30, 1863.

James Ralston Amos, letter to Walter Lowrie, February 7, 1863.

James Ralston Amos, letter to Walter Lowrie, February n.d., 1863.

James Ralston Amos, letter to Walter Lowrie, April 3, 1863.

James Ralston Amos, letter to Walter Lowrie, May 5, 1863.

James Ralston Amos, letter to Walter Lowrie, July 1, 1863.

James Ralston Amos, letter to Walter Lowrie, July 8, 1863.

James Ralston Amos, letter to Walter Lowrie, August 26, 1863.

James Ralston Amos, letter to Walter Lowrie, November 10, 1863.

James Ralston Amos, letter to Walter Lowrie, March 14, 1864.

Thomas Henry Amos, letter to Walter Lowrie, April 30, 1863.

Thomas Henry Amos, letter to Walter Lowrie, June 2, 1863.

Thomas Henry Amos, letter to Walter Lowrie, June 8, 1863.

Thomas Henry Amos, letter to Walter Lowrie, September 28, 1863.

Thomas Henry Amos, letter to Walter Lowrie, February 27, 1864.

Thomas Henry Amos, letter to Walter Lowrie, April 4, 1864.

Thomas Henry Amos, letter to Walter Lowrie, nd., 1864.

Thomas Henry Amos, letter to Walter Lowrie, July 18, 1864.

Thomas Henry Amos, letter to Walter Lowrie, July 24, 1865.

Thomas Henry Amos, letter to John C. Lowrie, October 26, 1865.

Thomas Henry Amos, letter to John C. Lowrie, November 2, 1865.

Thomas Henry Amos, letter to John C. Lowrie, May 25, 1866.

Thomas Henry Amos, letter to John C. Lowrie, January 30, 1867.

Thomas Henry Amos, letter to John C. Lowrie, February n.d., 1867.

Thomas Henry Amos, letter to John B. Pinney, October 25, 1867.

Thomas Henry Amos, letter to John C. Lowrie, February 1, 1869.

Thomas Henry Amos, letter to John C. Lowrie, April 7, 1869.

Thomas Henry Amos, letter to John C. Lowrie, April 13 & May 11, 1869.

Thomas Henry Amos, letter to John C. Lowrie, May 7, 1869.

Thomas Henry Amos, letter to John C. Lowrie, May 18, 1869.

Edward Wilmot Blyden, letter to John C. Lowrie, July 12, 1869.

Hopkins W. Erskine, letter to John C. Lowrie, July 12, 1869.

Hopkins W. Erskine, letter to John C. Lowrie, August 11, 1869.

H.D. Brown, letter to William Rankin, Jr., August 18, 1869.

Acknowledgments

The works of persons whom I will never meet have made this book possible. Scholar-President Horace Mann Bond's exhaustive study of Lincoln University's history and Paul and Marianne Russo's path finding research of Hinsonville are invaluable starting points for understanding the role of the Amos brothers in founding Lincoln and shaping its distinctive legacy.

I owe a special debt of gratitude to Langston Hughes Memorial Library colleagues who went out of their way to help gather and prepare material for this work: Doris Hughes, Neal Carlson, Brenda Snider, Sophia Sotilleo, Ugochi Nwachuku, Bonnie Horn, and Elizabeth Pitt; and to archivists and librarians of the Presbyterian Historical Society, Chester County Historical Society, Delaware Historical Society, Charles L. Blockson Afro-American Collection of Temple University and Schomburg Center for Research in Black Culture.

I am equally grateful to Thomas Henry Amos descendants Ernest Levister and Yvonne Gipson for sharing detailed family documents which uniquely enrich this story; and friends and members of Hosanna who actively support efforts to educate the public about the church's role in American history. Edith Jones, direct descendant of the Draper and Walls families of Hinsonville, and Hosanna pastor Thomas Warren--thanks to both of you for indulging my unquenchable fascination with the Hosanna's relationship to Lincoln University.

Sincere thanks to members of the Faculty Research and Publication Committee, Professor Levi A. Nwachuku, and to President Robert R. Jennings for directly supporting this effort to uncover a distinctive period of Lincoln's history.

And to James and Thomas for patiently waiting 155 years to be heard: May your stories continually instruct and inspire the beneficiaries of your sacrifices.

The Night is Far Spent, the Day is at Hand.

About the Author

Cheryl Renée Gooch is Dean of the College of Arts, Humanities and Social Sciences at The Lincoln University. A former journalist, she teaches, conducts research and publishes in the areas of journalism history, ethnographic journalism, and communication and social change.

Dr. Gooch can be contacted at cgooch@lincoln.edu.